Joan of Arc

Joan of Arc

Kathleen Kudlinski

DK PUBLISHING

LONDON, NEW YORK, MUNICH,
MELBOURNE, and DELHI

Editor : John Searcy
Publishing Director : Beth Sutinis
Designer : Mark Johnson Davies
Cartographer : Ed Merritt
Art Director : Dirk Kaufman
Photo Research : Anne Burns Images
Production : Ivor Parker
DTP Designer : Kathy Farias

First American Edition, 2008

08 09 10 11 12 10 9 8 7 6 5 4 3 2 1
Published in the United States
by DK Publishing
375 Hudson Street
New York, New York 10014

DK books are available at special discounts
when purchased in bulk for sales
promotions, premiums, fund-raising,
or educational use. For details, contact:

DK Publishing Special Markets
375 Hudson Street
New York, New York 10014
SpecialSales@dk.com

A catalog record for this book is available
from the Library of Congress.

ISBN 978-0-7566-3526-8 (Paperback)
ISBN 978-0-7566-3527-5 (Hardcover)

Printed and bound in China
by South China Printing Co., Ltd.

Photography credits:

Front Cover by Corbis/Bettman
Back Cover by Art Resource/Giraudon/
Musée des Beaux Arts, France

Discover more at
www.dk.com

Contents

"We Are All Ruined!"

Early in the morning on Wednesday, May 30, 1431, the townspeople of Rouen, France, hurried into the Old Marketplace. Farmers' carts full of excited families streamed in through the gates. No one wanted to miss this show. Medieval people gathered like this whenever troops of traveling actors came to town and staged plays. They formed crowds around jugglers, minstrels, and puppeteers on market days, too. But public hangings, whippings, and beheadings were the most exciting of all. They gave townsfolk something to talk about for years.

The castle doors opened. "La Pucelle!" someone called out: "The Maid!" The crowd surged forward.

Instead of a woman, soldiers marched out of the castle. More men-at-arms moved in from the town and from across the bridge at the Seine River. Finally, 800 of them stood in formation: English soldiers, the Duke of Burgundy's army, and hired troops. They had been fighting together to overthrow the French king, Charles VII. This morning they would celebrate the death of their enemy's legendary hero. The sun glinted on their swords and highlighted the colorful patterns on their shields. Knights rode their huge horses though the crowds. The square filled with restless murmurs.

At last a line of church officials in black robes solemnly climbed the stairs to a newly built platform. A few English

6

dignitaries marched along in step. Bishop Pierre Cauchon looked triumphant as he spread his skinny arms, demanding

silence. He had been in charge of the trial of the Maid of Orléans, Joan of Arc. It had taken a year for him to complete the church-run inquisition, but he'd found her guilty at last. Now she would pay for her crimes.

Bakers, bankers, and mothers with babies pushed forward as the prisoner's death cart drove in. The Maid was pulled off, dragging ankle chains. Young boys wormed their way to the front to shake their fists or throw rotten turnips at her. But when they saw Joan, they just stared. With her plain slip, the Maid looked like a simple country girl. It was hard to believe this slim teenager had led armies of men into bloody battles against the English and their allies.

In this painting, which hangs in the Musée des Beaux-Arts in Rouen, Joan is paraded past the people of the town.

The clerics made long speeches calling her a dangerous heretic who

deliberately disobeyed church law. She had repented, they said, but then she had sinned again. For that, she had to die.

The crowd cheered. This was what they had come to see. Now things seemed to move very fast. The executioner hurried Joan up onto a platform. At its center stood a pole surrounded by firewood. A pointed paper cone was shoved on her head. While Joan prayed loudly to God, Mary, and Jesus, more chains bound her body to the stake. She pleaded for mercy and for a cross. A nearby Englishman quickly made one of sticks and handed it to her. Joan kissed it, then tucked it into the neck of her dress. A priest ran to the town's church, hurrying back with a tall cross used for processions. He held it above her.

Joan kept her eyes on the cross while a lit torch touched the firewood. At first, nothing happened. Then a thin wisp of smoke rose. Soon tongues of flame licked at the wood by Joan's feet. The Maid called out for Jesus as the flames danced up her dress and filled her hair. "Jesus!" she called again, her voice clear and strong. The paper cap crumpled into a crown of fire and the crowd and the soldiers went silent. Why wasn't the Maid screaming in agony? They could all see the horror of death by flame. They could hear it. They could smell it. Yet Joan simply called out to Jesus. She didn't curse. She said nothing against God, even in her final agonies.

People made the sign of the cross and turned away in horror. Women pulled their aprons over their faces. Grown men cried tears. "Jesus!" the Maid called out, clearly, six times. Then she was silent. At last Joan was dead, though the fire burned on, charring her limp body.

The square emptied silently. People did not want to meet each other's eyes. This was not entertainment. The English Royal Secretary muttered to his comrades, "We are all ruined, for a good and holy person was burned."

As the fire died, the executioner glared at the few onlookers until they wandered away. He stayed, guarding what was left of Joan's body. He poured oil on her remains and added extra wood to burn it all away. When only coals were left, the executioner stirred the ashes as they cooled. Finally he was satisfied.

He looked around to see if anyone was watching, then quickly gathered the ashes and carried them to the Seine. He sprinkled them into the river, pausing to smash bits of bone or teeth with a rock. He glanced over his shoulder again as Joan slipped downstream into history.

Joan looks heavenward as a priest holds a cross above her and a soldier adds more fuel to the deadly fire.

1

Dancing around the Fairy Tree

There was no wall protecting the French village of Domrémy, where Jehanne d'Arc (now known to us as Joan of Arc) was born around 1412. There were no calendars there, either. People in the Middle Ages measured their years by the series of church holy days. One source gives Joan's birthday as January 6, the Feast of the Epiphany, but the truth is that no one is really sure of the day, or even the year, that Jacques d'Arc and his wife, Isabelle, brought their daughter into the world.

At first, Joan was one of five children living in the d'Arc family home. Two married and left while she was young. That left Pierre and Jean. Keeping up with these two energetic boys made Joan strong, and a bit of a tomboy. Their teasing

Preserved for more than 500 years, Joan of Arc's childhood home still stands in Domrémy, France.

With its tall bell tower, the village church was the center of life in Domrémy when Joan was growing up.

helped her become quick-witted, too.

Her stone house was one of a handful of buildings clustered around a country church on the banks of the Meuse River. A few dozen farms dotted the rolling hills nearby. Out her back door, Joan could see her father's garden, the barn, and a pig wallow. Farm chores kept the three d'Arc children busy.

The church stood tall and proud next door to the d'Arcs' house. Bells rang loudly from its steeple several times every day, reminding people to pray. Since no one had clocks or watches, these church bells marked time for everyone. Joan loved the bells, except when they sounded alerts. Enemies could strike Domrémy at any time.

When the alarm sounded, Joan's father was in charge of hurrying people out of the village. As *doyen,* he held the keys to a nearby castle where villagers and their animals could take refuge behind thick, safe walls. The doyen was also in charge of collecting taxes and settling local disputes. It made Joan proud that her father was a leader. Everyone looked up to him.

One spring, Joan wandered out of town with her best friend, Hauviette, following a line of older girls and boys. They hiked through the hills to a huge old tree standing

11

alone in a field. Some teenagers showed the little girls how to weave necklaces of wildflowers and hang them on the "Fairy Tree." They recited poems, expressing their desire for kind, handsome husbands. Laughing, they joined hands and danced together under the tree. Most of the boys played games of chase and somersaulted in the soft green grass. Joan watched a few older boys join in the dancing, too. Then the laugher got even louder. Soon, they opened baskets of cheese and bread and wine for a midday meal.

Back at home, Joan's mother told her that she, too, had danced under the Fairy Tree. So had Joan's great-grandmother. Maidens had been dancing there in the spring as long as anybody could remember.

While they worked together, Isabelle taught young Joan the skills she would need as a girl in the Middle Ages. Joan sewed and wove cloth, milked cows, churned butter, and made cheese. She could kill a goose. She knew how to pluck its down feathers for pillows, and how to cook it for supper. But Joan never learned to read or write. Who would have guessed she would need those skills?

12

Joan did need to know all about the Roman Catholic Church. Its laws governed Medieval life in Europe. Just like the town or the state, the church had courts where people could be tried and punished for breaking its laws. Priests ran these ecclesiastical courts. The church had separate ecclesiastical jails, too, where they could punish people. Priests and bishops—and their ruler, the Pope—held real power. The church could raise armies and fight wars. And France was so completely a Christian country that it was hard to separate church from state.

Isabelle d'Arc helped her daughter learn the Catholic rules for life. She taught Joan the prayers she should say to God. The beautiful words and ideas filled the child's mind. Isabelle told Joan that shortly after she was born, she had been sprinkled with holy water in a

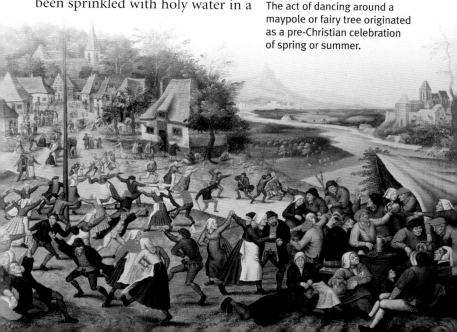

The act of dancing around a maypole or fairy tree originated as a pre-Christian celebration of spring or summer.

church. This baptism made her a member of the community of all Roman Catholics living anywhere on Earth. The church community included the souls of every faithful member who had ever died, too. These heavenly church members lived on forever with God, Jesus, and his mother, Mary, as well as all the angels and saints.

When Joan was about six, her mother helped her prepare for a sacrament called communion. Before she could practice this very holy ritual, Joan had to be purified. In private, she confessed to a priest all the ways she had broken church rules. He told her how to make up for her sins. She followed his instructions. Then, that night, Joan stopped eating. Her mother told her that fasting, or choosing not to eat, was one way to show her faith in God.

By morning of the next day, Joan felt a little hungry, but she also felt clean and light and holy. Only then, at a ceremony called mass, could she eat a wafer of bread known as the Eucharist. Joan's mother told her the bread had become the body of Jesus, the son of God. Joan believed this with all her heart. She "received the sacrament of

The Catholic Church

The Roman Catholic Church is the community of Christians who look to the pope (also called the bishop of Rome) as their spiritual leader. In Joan's time, the church was the dominant force in Western Europe, and the pope was more powerful than many kings. Today, the church's power has lessened, but it still has more than a billion members worldwide, many of them in Latin America, Africa, and Asia.

the Eucharist despite her young age," Isabelle d'Arc said later, "and gave herself to fasting and prayer with great devotion and fervor." Throughout her childhood, Joan went to the church next door whenever mass was offered.

Communion wafers are used to re-enact the Last Supper where Jesus shared bread with his followers.

At church, she gazed at statues and pictures of saints. These people were heroes recognized by the church. Their faith went so far beyond the ordinary that they could do exceptional, even miraculous, things on earth. They all went to heaven. Many of the most popular saints of the Medieval era, such as Saint Catherine and Saint Margaret, were martyrs. They'd been killed back when the Roman Empire was trying to stamp out the young Christian church. By living and dying in such devout ways, the saints served as role models for ordinary people struggling to lead Christian lives.

Joan loved hearing stories of the saints. Saint Catherine was a young Christian maiden from a wealthy family in Alexandria, Egypt. The emperor Maximinus punished the early Christians brutally because they worshipped their own god. They refused to worship him. Catherine journeyed to the Roman palaces. She stood alone in the throne room and challenged the emperor and his court. She scolded them for being cruel. She announced that the old gods they worshipped were false.

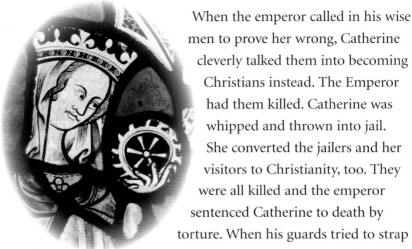

When the emperor called in his wise men to prove her wrong, Catherine cleverly talked them into becoming Christians instead. The Emperor had them killed. Catherine was whipped and thrown into jail. She converted the jailers and her visitors to Christianity, too. They were all killed and the emperor sentenced Catherine to death by torture. When his guards tried to strap her to a huge torture wheel, it broke apart at her touch. To silence her, the emperor finally had her head cut off.

Saint Catherine holds a tiny torture wheel in this stained-glass window, dating from the mid-14th century.

Joan knew Saint Margaret's story, too. Like Catherine, Margaret was a young maiden who vowed never to marry so she could focus her life on worshiping Jesus. As a shepherdess, Margaret spent her days praying in the fields while her sheep grazed. When a Roman official demanded that she become his wife and worship his gods, Margaret refused. The official then put Margaret on trial for clinging to her Christian faith.

In court, Margaret spoke bluntly. She said that Jupiter, Venus, and all the rest of the Roman gods were false. There was only one God, she said, and his son was Jesus. The gods the Romans had worshipped for centuries simply did not exist.

People in the room leapt to their feet, shouting in outrage. Margaret was sentenced to death. The flames of a fire did not

RELIC

A relic is a part of a saint's body, or an object from her life, which is treated as a sacred artifact.

burn her. Tied hand and foot, she was dropped into a huge cauldron of boiling water. The ties broke and Margaret stood up, unharmed. Finally she was beheaded—but she never broke her vow to God.

The lives of these saints inspired Joan. She felt as if she knew these brave young women. One of Saint Catherine's bones was still kept in a chapel in France. There were pieces of Saint Margaret's body saved in churches, too. To Joan, these long-treasured relics proved that the saints were very real.

The saints also seemed close. In life, they had worked miracles. People thought they could still work miracles from heaven. Whenever a lamb went missing, townspeople prayed to Saint Margaret, asking her to help them find it. Young women prayed to Saint Catherine, asking for help finding a good husband. They still searched hard for lost lambs and happy marriages, but it felt good to think someone in heaven might be helping.

This 16th-century image of Saint Margaret comes from a series of connected panels, designed to be contemplated by churchgoers.

17

2

A Country Divided

Although Joan's childhood was happy, it was a happiness that took place in a war zone. By the time she was born, England and France had been battling for almost 70 years. English kings wanted the rich farmlands of France. They wanted the wine country, the ports, and the fortresslike cities. They wanted the taxes they could collect on all this wealth.

The King of France, Charles VI, was no help in the fight. He was so mentally ill that he could not rule. The French people were ashamed of their king and worried for their future. The Count of Armagnac stepped in

Although this illustration shows only swords and spears, the English mainly used longbows at Agincourt.

to take over, leading the French loyalists (now known as Armagnacs) against their English occupiers.

When Joan was three, news of a terrible battle reached her village. Henry V, the king of England, had invaded France at the city of Agincourt. It took only 7,000 English soldiers to defeat 20,000 French troops. French people everywhere were humiliated.

Henry V of England grew up as a king and knew how to use power. His confidence shows in this portrait.

The French Duke of Burgundy chose to work with the English. He and the mad king's wife signed the Treaty of Troyes, written by Bishop Pierre Cauchon, which made the king of England the ruler of France as well. As a powerful noble, the duke controlled not only the territory of Burgundy but also its neighbor, Champagne. Now he encouraged his subjects to submit to the rule of the strong, sane English king, Henry V. A civil war followed, with the English-friendly Burgundian forces fighting the loyal Armagnacs.

Domrémy sat in a contested area. The town officially fell under the Duke of Burgundy's rule, but its people were fiercely loyal to the French Armagnac cause. Joan's family, the d'Arcs, hated England. Like their neighbors, they wanted a free France. Joan heard the talk at the dinner table. She heard it on the street. People from neighboring towns, all Burgundian, made raids into the village or beat up Domrémy's citizens whenever they could.

The French called Charles VI "the Mad King." Today's psychologists think he suffered from schizophrenia.

The Armagnacs believed in France as a free nation. They treasured their language and customs. They knew their glorious history. Armagnacs still believed in the ancient line of French kings. Charles VI might not be fit to rule, but he did have a son who was next in line for the crown. The young Prince Charles was 23, old enough to become king. Until then, his status as dauphin gave him land and a small income of his own. The dauphin was in no hurry to take the French crown. His counselors told him to wait until things settled down. The whole country was a war zone, they argued, and too dangerous to take control of. The young Charles agreed. He lived comfortably in a walled city named Chinon. He was surrounded by friends there. He did not have to make decisions or take risks.

Meanwhile, neither Charles nor the Duke of Burgundy put much effort into law enforcement. Bands of thieves roamed the land. Near border towns like Domrémy, bandits lay in wait along the main roads. These highwaymen preyed on travelers. Joan often saw her neighbors stagger home cut and bruised. Some died. Others simply disappeared.

In 1422 Joan heard that the mad king Charles VI had died. The dauphin made no move to take over the throne. The powerful English king Henry died that year, too. His son was still a baby, but he was crowned anyway, as Henry VI. His advisors named his uncle, the Duke of Bedford, a wealthy and battle-hardened Englishman, to rule France in the boy king's place.

Years of war had worn down the French spirit. Believing in the glory of a free France was hard when the country looked like a battlefield. Their own king didn't seem to want to rule. The war-weary people yearned for something to restore their hope before it was too late.

This map shows the divided loyalty of France around the year 1430, when Joan was leading her armies.

England

English Channel

Agincourt
Beaurevoir
Rouen   Soissens
Compiègne   Paris Reims
Seine   Vaucouleurs   Nancy
         Troyes Domrémy
Orléans Auxerre
Blois Gien
Loire Tours Dijon
Chinon Loches
Poitiers

ATLANTIC
OCEAN

Holy Roman Empire

France

Bordeaux

Garonne
Toulouse

Rhône

Castile

Navarre

Mediterranean
Sea

Aragon

Map Key

English/Burgundian territory

Armagnac territory

0 miles   100   200
0 km   100   200   300

chapter **3**

Voices

Joan's days were filled with chores. She led cows up into
the sunny meadows to graze. She threw kitchen slops to
the pig and scraps to the chickens. Beetles had to be picked
off the garden plants. Joan plowed the fields. She hoed,
weeded, and hauled buckets of water from the well. Every
day, she pushed the waste out through the trough in the
middle of her house's dirt floor to the gutter by the road.

All the village girls carried spindles in their apron pockets for spinning yarn. They carried long forked sticks called distaffs over their shoulders. These sticks held wads of fluffy wool the girls had cut from their sheep, then washed and combed.

Hay was cut by hand and then raked into haystacks in the 1400s. Even in the field, girls and women wore dresses.

Whenever their hands were empty for a few moments, they spun yarn.

Joan and her friends Mengette and Hauviette often sat together in the sunshine, spinning. Joan would reach one hand up to tease wool fibers off the tangle atop her distaff. She gently pulled, twisted, and turned the soft wool between her fingers until it formed out a strong length of yarn. As a little child, spinning had been frustrating; her yarn uneven. By the time Joan was ten, it was a soothing action she could do perfectly without thought.

Spinning with a distaff was woman's work. Today, "the distaff side" still refers to the mother's side of the family.

Sometimes Joan spun by candlelight in her home, listening to her parents' worries. There was always the chance of attack. Did everyone in the village know what to do? Would a deadly sickness strike again? Would the young dauphin ever take the crown so France would have its own king? Every evening, Joan's parents prayed aloud for answers, for hope, and for strength. They spoke to God. They pleaded with the saints for help. Before every meal they blessed the food they'd been given. At night they thanked the Lord for their day. Speaking to the powers in heaven seemed as normal to Joan as talking to her own family.

Joan's simple home was heated by fireplaces. Today, a tile floor has been added over the original packed dirt.

When Joan heard the bells ring from the church tower, she ran to worship. The bell ringer later described a time when he forgot to do his job: "Joan caught up with me and chided me, saying that I had not done well." He said she promised to bring him little gifts if he would be more faithful to his job.

Deep in the oak woods up in the hills stood a rustic chapel named Notre-Dame-de-Bermont. Joan walked up to the simple building almost every Saturday. She felt close to God in the hush under the huge, old oak trees. She stepped inside, crossed herself, and knelt at the altar. Sometimes she lit candles and prayed silently; sometimes she spoke aloud.

Joan often sensed the angels and saints near her when she stood in the middle of the pasture under the huge bowl of blue sky. Jean Waterin, a plow boy a little older than Joan, later recalled: "Often when we were playing together, Joan would go away from us a little and often spoke with God, it seemed to me."

Joan tried to imagine what the shepherdess Saint Margaret would say to her across the ages. The saint had known the smell of wet sheep's wool. She'd heard the bleating of newborn lambs. Joan pictured whole conversations with the ancient martyr about sheep. About life on a farm. About keeping strange men away. Joan also imagined the clever things Saint Catherine's high-bred voice might say. Over and over, when her hands were busy but her mind was not, Joan thought about her favorite saints.

One day, when she was about 13, Joan sat in her father's garden. It was a warm morning like so many others. Her eyes were unfocused. She let her mind go empty and tried to summon the saints she knew so well.

A sudden flash of light seared her eyes. Blinded, Joan reached out her arms, trying to get her bearings. Her breath came in frightened gasps. What was happening to her?

Joan could have seen this painting, which depicts a Roman official coming upon Saint Margaret in a pasture.

Somewhere out in the darkness, she heard a powerful male voice: "Joan," it called. "Joan!"

"Papa?" she answered. As her vision cleared she realized that her father was not there. Neither was her brother. There were no men in the garden at all. Who could have called? Fear filled Joan. Was she hearing things? Joan prayed aloud for guidance.

She tried to remember if any of her friends heard voices like this. The priest had told Bible stories about men who heard God's voice. Through the ages, faithful people had heard God speak. Others had reported seeing the Virgin Mary or other saints visiting here on earth. Had Joan had one of these visitations? Her practical mind said no, but the skin shivered on her arms. Something had happened. Joan's chest went tight with fear.

Over the next few weeks Joan listened for the voice. She couldn't help herself. In the pasture, she made her mind blank and focused on angels. In church, in bed, and in the oak woods, she prayed for another word from on high. And she listened.

Even Joan's parents noticed how much she daydreamed. They worried that she had fallen in love.

In Christianity, the archangel Michael was responsible for driving Satan out of heaven, after he rebelled against God.

Sometimes she heard nothing. A few times she heard a distant echo. "Joan," it called to her. She got better at picking the voice out of the clutter of farm sounds, or the river babbling, or even her father snoring in the loft. Who could it be?

Then one morning, as she sat daydreaming, she looked up and saw the archangel Michael standing right beside her. Michael was an important commander in God's army. He was tall and strong and carrying the sword he used to battle Satan. The angel seemed as real to her as the sheep up on the ridge. Fear shook Joan until her teeth chattered. Michael said soothing things in his familiar deep, sweet voice.

Soon Joan had visits from Saint Catherine and Saint Margaret, too, as clear as day. She could talk to them in her mind, just as she did when she was pretending—but this felt very different. She didn't have to ask why they'd chosen her. She had a calling. Joan prayed her thanks to God but kept the miracle secret.

A holy calling had to be answered, Joan knew. When she had asked her priest about visitations, he had talked to her for hours about this. As the seasons passed, Joan fasted and prayed and talked with her saints.

Finally, she realized what they wanted her to do. Joan remembered how often her mother and father had prayed for the dauphin to grow up and act like a king. Maybe her voices wanted her to help her parents' prayers come true.

That was it! The saints had come to tell her to go and help the dauphin prepare to lead his country. More, Joan thought, standing tall in the field, I am to make sure he is

In this image, the archangel Michael, Saint Margaret, and Saint Catherine, are depicted as ghostly forms as they speak to Joan.

crowned! She fell to her knees in the grass and prayed her thanks. Joan kept her heavenly voices secret for many months. She got even quieter and more pious. Her parents worried about the change.

When Joan was about 14, her parents decided it was time for her to get married. They had picked out a groom for her and announced the engagement in church. But the voices had said nothing about getting married! A desperate Joan persuaded her parents to end her engagement. God had bigger

In medieval marriage ceremonies, brides wore red. Our familiar white bridal gowns date only from the 1800s.

things for her to do. To anyone who asked, Joan said she had dedicated her body to God. Like nuns, priests, and many of the saints, she vowed never to become physically intimate with another person. It made Joan seem holy. She would be forever a maid, chaste and untouched.

At last, Joan was sure enough to tell people about the miracles that were happening to her. It was awkward at first. She tried hinting at the truth to her friend Michel Lebuin. "Once she told me," he remembered, "that there was a maid, between Coussey and Vaucouleurs, who before a year was out would have the king of France anointed."

Michel didn't understand what she meant at all. Joan began telling others that the archangel Michael, Saint Margaret, and Saint Catherine had told her to go to the dauphin. It was up to her to get him crowned. Most people doubted her. But they all knew the stories of angels coming to earth. The village priest had heard her confessions for years. Her reports of voices never changed. She was so driven to take action that the priest finally admitted that she might be divinely inspired.

chapter 4

The Maid from the Oak Forest

When she was about 16, Joan's uncle agreed to take her to see Robert de Baudricourt, the captain of loyal forces in the nearby town of Vaucouleurs. Baudricourt knew the dauphin. He could give Joan a letter of introduction to carry with her when she went to Chinon. After reading the letter, the dauphin's guards were sure to let Joan into the castle to see Charles. Baudricourt could also arrange safe passage to Chinon where the dauphin was staying. Between the highwaymen and the Burgundians, any road trip was dangerous. To discourage attacks, Joan wore a man's jacket of red wool over her dress, along with a man's hat.

The medieval church still stands in Vaucouleurs, along with a fragment of the city's original stone walls.

Accompanied by her uncle and two of Baudricourt's men, Joan soon reached the walls of Vaucouleurs. She told everyone she met that she was destined to have the dauphin crowned King Charles VII. Most of the people who heard her story just laughed.

For days, Robert de Baudricourt made Joan and her men wait. On May 13, 1428, he finally let her into the castle. Joan swallowed hard. She had never seen such wealth. She passed through a pair of vast wooden doors. Beneath her shoes she felt a floor of stone, not dirt. The walls were stone too, covered by brightly woven rugs. These tapestries showed scenes of battles.

"Yes?" Baudricourt's voice was impatient. Joan could only stare at him. The man was sitting on a real chair, not just a bench like normal people used. It made him look so important.

Suddenly Joan remembered Saint Catherine, standing bold and persuasive in the emperor's court. Joan felt flooded with power. She stood straight and tall, telling Robert de Baudricourt about the voices. She reported what they had told her—she was to crown the king.

The courtiers around Baudricourt laughed aloud at Joan's story. Baudricourt smirked. He told her uncle to take Joan home and give her a slap or two to end her foolishness. Joan's face burned as her uncle hurried her out of the room.

The trip home passed safely, but within two months Domrémy was attacked by Burgundians. Jacques d'Arc led

The Duke of Orléans lived in relative comfort during his imprisonment in England, even composing several poems.

everyone a few miles down the road to safety in the walled city nearby. From the towers and parapets, Joan and Hauviette watched the smoke rise from their village.

With the support of England, the Burgundians had been fighting for more territory for months. Besides Domrémy, they had attacked a string of other small villages. The prize they wanted, though, was Orléans. This large walled city stood on the Loire River at the intersection of several major roads connecting the north and south of France. Whoever held Orléans controlled these main trade routes.

The city's leader, the Duke of Orléans, was a prisoner in England. He had been captured at the Battle of Agincourt. Since 1427, his younger brother John of Dunois had filled in as ruler. Dunois and his loyal Frenchmen had been holding off Burgundian attacks for months. Reinforcements came from England now and then. Fresh soldiers trickled in from the French side, too. Under English commanders, the Burgundian troops seemed to be winning.

Finally, these English forces controlled all but one of the gates into the city. They'd built small forts, called *bastides,* alongside every road leading in. A troop of soldiers lived in each bastide. More troops were camped nearby in tents or homes they had taken over. No one could get past them to help the loyal Frenchmen in Orléans. By October 12, 1428, this siege was in place.

Joan knew about the siege of Orléans. Everyone was guessing how soon the city would fall to the English. The long war seemed almost over and France was losing. People prayed for a miracle to save their country.

Out in the field with the animals, Joan fretted. Saint Catherine had made it clear: It was up to Joan to make sure that the dauphin was crowned. He needed to undergo the ancient, traditional ceremony, affirming that his rule was sanctioned by God. In addition, Joan's voices now told her she had a more active role to play in the salvation of her country: She needed to lift the siege of Orléans. Only then could the dauphin be crowned, and only then could the English finally be driven out of France.

When Baudricourt sent her home in May, she had agreed to drop the whole idea of seeing the dauphin. She didn't talk about it anymore. But all around her people began taking her claims of heavenly voices seriously. Many remembered an old prophecy that France would be saved by a pure young maiden from the oak forest. People whispered that Joan might be the one.

SIEGE

A siege is a military operation in which a city is encircled and blockaded by an opposing army, in an attempt to force the city to surrender.

The Nobility

In the Middle Ages, the nobility, or nobles, were people with inherited land and titles (such as *duke* or *baron*). They enjoyed many privileges that ordinary people did not. During times of war, nobles supported their king by raising and commanding private armies, since most countries didn't have unified national militaries.

A huge stand of ancient oak trees could be seen from the d'Arc's fields. Joan had walked away from a marriage, so she was still a maiden. She had insisted that she was sent by God.

By this point, French loyalists were so discouraged that they were eager to grasp at any trace of hope. Excited rumors spread throughout the countryside. In Orléans, John of Dunois heard that the legendary Maid was coming to protect his city. Even the dauphin heard the gossip.

Joan traveled with her family to see Robert de Baudricourt again. He refused to meet with her, so her family got a room in an inn to wait. Joan told everyone of her mission. A sick old duke living in the nearby town of Nancy sent for Joan. When she traveled to his home, the nobleman asked for her blessing. He was treating her as if she were already a saint who could work miracles.

Startled, Joan laughed, and said she could not cure him. She did pray for him, though. Like Saint Catherine, she scolded him about his morals. She also said he should send his son with her to fight for France. The son returned with Joan to Vaucouleurs where she waited impatiently to see Baudricourt. Joan even set out on her own once to see the dauphin. Many miles down the road, she changed her mind. She was supposed to see Baudricourt first. The voices had been clear about that.

Joan sent another message demanding to be seen. This time, Robert let her into his court. To test her, Baudricourt had a priest perform an exorcism. This ceremony is designed to cast any demons out of a person. Nothing happened to Joan, so Baudricourt decided she was neither a sorceress nor a witch.

In February of 1429, he finally sent Joan to the dauphin with a letter of introduction. He also gave her a sword and a high-bred horse. She surprised everyone by riding well. Baudricourt sent along an escort of four mounted soldiers to guard her. For extra protection, Joan dressed entirely in men's clothes. She also cut her dark hair short, like a boy's.

In this Italian depiction of an exorcism, a woman falls to the floor as a demon is cast out of her body by a priest.

This painting shows Joan accepting a sword and introduction to the dauphin as she leaves Vaucouleurs mounted on her new horse.

She didn't want to attract any man's attention. She had promised her body to God. The voices had told her to.

The trip from Vaucouleurs to Chinon took 11 days. Part of the route was through enemy territory. Joan and her companions traveled mostly at night. They avoided the roads. It was early spring in France, so the many rivers they crossed in the dark were running high. Joan kept hurrying everyone on. Her voices told her she only had until midsummer to crown the dauphin, and that couldn't happen until she'd gotten the siege lifted from Orléans. The voices had foretold her death, too, though Joan seldom talked about that. "I shall last one year, hardly more," she admitted once. It wasn't much time to save a country.

But first, she insisted on stopping at a church. Joan had crossed into territory loyal to the dauphin now, and she was welcomed everywhere. In the town of Sainte-Catherine-de-Fierbois she sent a message ahead to the dauphin telling him she was coming. Then she attended mass at the chapel that

PILGRIMAGE

A pilgrimage is a journey to a sacred place, thought to aid in one's spiritual growth.

had given the town its name. Seven hundred years earlier, a famous crusader had left his battle sword there. No one knew where that treasure had gone.

More significantly, around 1400, another French crusader had visited the tomb of Saint Catherine in the Sinai. He brought back a priceless silver box that supposedly contained relics of the saint. This silver reliquary was said to hold actual pieces of Catherine's body, saved since her death. They were withered, black, and ugly, but they were considered to be absolute proof that she had lived. Thousands of people made pilgrimages to Sainte-Catherine-de-Fierbois to pray in the presence of her remains.

Joan's party moved on. They settled into the little town of Chinon, nestled at the base of the soaring walls of the castle. As always, she was in a hurry to set out on her mission. The dauphin kept her waiting for two full days, while his messengers and counselors demanded to hear the details of her plan. She refused to say anything except to the dauphin himself. "He shall have no help if not through me," she warned them.

Reliquaries were often works of art. This chest of precious metal and intricate enamel dates back to the 1100s.

chapter **5**

Meeting the King

At last, on the afternoon of March 6, 1429, the dauphin's messengers came for Joan. They carried torches to light her way up the steep road. Inside the castle, more torches made the night as light as day. Coming from little Domrémy, Joan had never seen so many torches lit indoors, so many elegantly dressed people, or such an incredible display of wealth. Colorful tapestries lined the stone walls. Musicians and jugglers strolled about to entertain the crowd. The dauphin had planned it this way. He expected the little country shepherdess to be overwhelmed by his display of wealth. Three hundred people filled the great hall, but no one was seated up on the raised platform that held his throne.

LE TRESVICTORIEVX ROY DE FRANCE

CHARLES · SEPTIESME · DE CE NOM

The self-conscious dauphin dressed to cover his flaws. Here he wears puffy sleeves to hide sloping shoulders.

This medieval illustration of Joan meeting the dauphin gets many details wrong, but captures the importance of the moment.

The dauphin was on the floor mingling with his guests. The 26-year-old Charles was shy about meeting new people. Skinny and clumsy, he wore extra long robes to cover his slightly crooked legs. His nose was big and his chin was small. The dauphin hated seeing people's first reactions to his looks. Besides, he thought it would be amusing to watch Joan's confusion as she searched for him. His plan would make her look helpless to his friends instead of mysteriously powerful. She couldn't know what he looked like. Charles tried to melt into the crowd.

Joan calmly scanned the room. Then she walked directly to the dauphin and curtsied smoothly. "God give you life, gentle king," she said. The court historian recorded the exchange.

"What if I am not the king, Joan?" he teased, pointing to someone nearby. "There is the king."

"In God's name, gentle prince," she answered. "It is you and no other."

"I am Joan the Maid," Joan told the Dauphin, as she confessed it later to her priest, "and the King of Heaven commands that through me you be anointed and crowned in the city of Reims . . . "

Even when Joan had finally convinced the dauphin that her voices were real, many in his court did not believe her.

Charles did not completely believe her until she revealed her knowledge of a secret that, he later said, only God would have known. To this day, we don't know what this secret was, but Joan's words had such an effect on the dauphin that he immediately announced that she was to live in the castle with him. He assigned a young servant, Louis de Coutes, to work as her page, helping her however she needed.

In the castle's tower, Louis watched Joan. "I often saw her on her knees praying," he later testified. "I could never hear what she was saying, even though sometimes she wept." He also saw many men visit and talk with Joan. By night women stood guard to make sure no one bothered her.

One nobleman, the Duke of Alençon, believed Joan completely. He liked her, too. Joan was confident and forceful, with a fiery temper and a sharp tongue when crossed. With her skinny body and boy's clothing and haircut,

PAGE

A page was a boy who served as the assistant to a knight or other distinguished person.

40

Joan did not look anything like other teenage girls at court. Under it all, the Duke of Alençon could see that she was an innocent country girl. He gave her a beautiful horse to ride on her journeys. More importantly, he became her friend.

A few days later, the whole royal party took Joan to Poitiers, a day-long journey. Joan had convinced Charles that her claims were true. But there were many others around the dauphin who did not believe her. She could be possessed by devils, they said. She might be be a spy, a liar, or completely insane. They insisted that Joan's background be checked. In Poitiers, she was repeatedly questioned by priests and professors about her faith and her voices. She began to see how much Charles leaned on others for advice.

They all returned to Chinon, then she was sent back to Poitiers for a more official trial. For three weeks she answered questions from Bible experts, archbishops, professors, priests, and more. Though

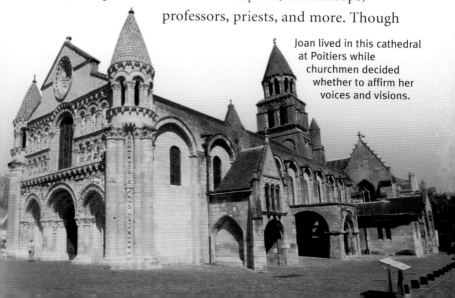

Joan lived in this cathedral at Poitiers while churchmen decided whether to affirm her voices and visions.

In the Middle Ages, clerics wore dramatic clothing. A monk, an archbishop, and a priest are pictured here.

Joan was impatient to get moving again, she answered every question carefully. Saint Catherine's example helped. Joan astonished her judges. She even surprised herself. Joan could neither read nor write. She had never gone to school. How could she outsmart these learned men?

Friar Seguin, a priest, asked Joan what exactly the voices told her. Seguin reported that Joan was clear and sure in her four-part answer. To begin with, "the city of Orléans would be free of the English," Joan had said, "but first she would send them an invitation to surrender." "Next, she said that the king would be consecrated at Reims." Third, Paris's loyalty would return to the king of France. And the Duke of Orléans would return from England where he was being held prisoner. Nothing could shake her strange certainty. There was no evidence that she was lying, either.

At last the dauphin could accept her help. He assigned another page, Raymond, and two heralds to serve her. Joan

HERALD

A herald was a personal messenger. In battles, heralds were immune from attack.

was also given five enormous war horses and several lighter trotters to use in the campaign to free Orléans. Two squires tended to her horses. The dauphin paid everyone's salaries and provided food, clothing, and shelter. Joan's brothers Pierre and Jean joined her company, too.

Joan began to train with the troops. She would need their loyalty in the battles to come. Once they got over the wonder of seeing a female soldier, they were all astonished by her strength and speed. She was a quick learner, too, handling weapons on foot and on horseback. Joan fearlessly played war games with the men, often besting seasoned fighters.

Excitement spread throughout France as stories about Joan were told in taverns, churches, marketplaces, and schools. People began to believe they had a chance to overthrow the English. Dozens and then hundreds of men arrived at Chinon from the countryside. They wanted to fight with the Maid.

They all marched to the town of Tours, where the rest of the loyalist army was gathering.

The only way to teach mounted soldiers like Joan how to fight was to practice with horses in the training ring.

6

The Sword in the Soil

As an official part of the dauphin's army, Joan needed to be outfitted for battle. A suit of shining white armor was forged for her in Tours, sized exactly for her small teenage body. Under the armor, she wore a suit of chain mail. This form-fitting garment was made entirely of metal links. It was designed to stop any arrows or swords that slid between the cracks of her armor. Joan had a helmet, too, to protect her head from rocks dropped from walls and other dangers of battle.

Next, Joan ordered a banner. It was no simple stitched design. Instead she asked for a painting that included Jesus and Mary, plus God being presented with a fleur-de-lis by kneeling angels. This, she would carry into battle.

Now Joan asked for someone to go back to Sainte-Catherine-de-Fierbois. Her voices had told her

Joan's jointed armor cost as much as 1,000 battle horses and weighed more than 35 pounds (16 kg).

that her battle sword would be found there, buried a few inches deep either in front of or behind the altar of the church. "It would be rusted," she said, "with five crosses engraved on it." The churchmen knew of no such sword. The townspeople thought the crusader's sword was just a legend. But the weapon showed up just as Joan had said. With a few gentle wipes, its thick rust fell away to reveal five crosses. The people of Saint-Catherine-de-Fierbois gave

Fleur-de-Lis

The fleur-de-lis (literally, "flower of the lily") is an ancient symbol of France and its king. According to legend, it was adopted by the first French king, Clovis I, after his conversion to Christianity in the year 496.

her a sheath for the sword, made out of gold fabric or velvet. Joan had another one made of tough leather.

Word of this miracle spread along with the news that the Maid was now a soldier, outfitted to do battle for France. She had announced that the dauphin would be king by midsummer, too—only three months away. Impossible, people thought, but wouldn't it be wonderful? More volunteers arrived to fight with her. They stayed without pay, finding their own food and using their own weapons.

Comment la pucelle batte deux filles

This symbolic illustration shows Joan physically chasing the camp followers away from her soldiers.

Joan's actions kept everyone talking. She rode among her men often, watching and encouraging them. With the dauphin's permission, she started to make changes. The soldiers, she insisted, must go to confession and take communion weekly, if not more often. France, she reminded them, was a Catholic country. Everyone should practice the official religion.

To make it convenient for the men, Joan had another banner made featuring a painting of Jesus on the cross. She enlisted a company of priests to carry it alongside the troops. Whenever they stopped—for the night, for meals, or for battle—the clerics hoisted this banner. Soldiers all knew they could meet by the banner to make confession or receive mass.

When Joan joined the army, there were many women following the troops, living in the tents or camping nearby. This was true of all armies. Some of these women were soldiers' wives. Others worked as cooks or laundry maids. Many just hung around for a chance to earn money as prostitutes. Joan insisted that all the women go home.

She demanded that the men clean up their bodies and their language, too. She even forbade cursing and crude talk. There was a lot of grumbling at first, but all these changes made an amazing difference in the ranks. For a change, the men were united under something holy and pure. Joan inspired them to be something better than they had been.

The whole country began to remember the greatness of France.

At the grand banquet held before the army left for Orléans, Joan sat at the head table near the dauphin. So did his advisors and generals. Each general had his own army, men he fed and paid. The soldiers often came from lands that the generals held as dukes or counts. Taxes from the land supported the noblemen and their personal armies. Some of these men were knights, sworn to fight for their king. Others had signed treaties or just agreed with the king's interests—for now. Most of them were troubled by the idea of a woman soldier having an army of her own.

She could see the whispering and glances cast her way. Joan had

These drawings of Joan's battle standard (top), pennant (left), and religious banner (right) are based on eyewitness accounts.

Longbows like this stood about six feet (2 m) tall. In Joan's time they were being replaced by crossbows.

been raised far from court. She was fierce about her calling, but sweet and honest about everything else. She had made enormous changes in the generals' armies. The soldiers loved her for it, but their leaders were jealous. The dauphin's advisors were worried, too, for their young leader had already begun to think of himself as king, and beyond their control. Joan did not yet know how ruthlessly people would fight to keep their power.

But the news from Orléans was bad. Few supplies were getting in. People there were nearly starving. Everyone at court knew they needed someone like Joan to help free this important city. Still, they schemed to make things hard for her.

The next morning, the armies marched to Blois, on the south side of the Loire River, about halfway to Orléans. They stopped at a French-controlled fortress there. Some soldiers filled supply wagons and carts with grain for people trapped in Orléans. Others rounded up hundreds of sheep, cows, pigs, and fowl to drive before them as they marched.

Around this time, Joan predicted that she would be wounded by an arrow above her breast. She said she would not die. Her voices had told her this, she said, and they would not lie.

As the troops rested and prepared for battle, Joan called for her herald and asked him to write down a message from her to King Henry VI of England. It seemed absurd that a 16-year-old farm girl would write directly to a powerful enemy king. It was even stranger that she might think he would read it. Joan's squire wrote down her words. "King of England . . . Surrender to the Maid," Joan demanded. "I am sent from God, the King of Heaven, to chase you out of all of France." Joan could neither write nor read what her squire had written. She could not even sign her own name. But she was the dauphin's official, so her orders were followed. On March 22, 1429, her herald carried the letter into the English camp.

The next day, the troops moved out with Joan in the lead, along with the captains and generals. They brought some supplies with them for Orléans, but left most of the food back at Blois. They needed to break through the siege

Symbolizing Henry VI's claims over England and France, this portrait features the English lion and French fleur-de-lis.

before they could deliver the massive herds and wagons full of grain. Joan could not wait to fight the British

Although Joan slept in full armor, this artist suggests she also had a guardian angel to protect her.

under their famous leader, John Talbot. She urged everyone to move faster. Joan had never traveled far from little Domrémy and she could not read maps. Robert of Baudricourt led them up the south side of the broad, deep river. It was a safe route through friendly territory. The company made good time.

As the only woman among thousands of men, Joan felt she needed to protect herself. The first night, she slept on the ground in her armor. She woke the next morning stiff, sore, and bruised. Day after day, she grew tougher—and crankier.

Joan was furious when she found out that hungry Orléans was on the north side of the Loire. They were standing with supplies on the south side. Only one narrow bridge crossed the river, and it was controlled by the English. All the soldiers, the supply carts, and the animals would have to be sailed across the river in boats! Worse, a strong wind had been blowing in the wrong direction for days. Sails would not work in this weather. Oarsmen could not row a big boat against the swift current and the wind, too. Joan felt helpless and betrayed.

John of Dunois, ruler of Orléans, rushed out of the city to meet with Joan. He had led a company of soldiers that very morning to divert the English attention. Talbot fought him at one of the English bastides. Dunois's forces had captured the fort and the English flag. It was their first victory in a long while, and Dunois was feeling proud. He had already brought the English battle flag back into Orléans to cheers and applause. He expected the same from Joan.

Instead, she stormed into him. "Are you the one who gave orders for me to come here on this side of the river, so that I could not go directly to Talbot and the English?"

Dunois admitted to choosing the route.

"I bring you better help than ever came to you from any soldier," Joan declared. "It is the help of the King of Heaven!"

At that very moment, the wind changed. Now boats could sail easily across the river.

Everyone stood silent. How could this have happened, they wondered. Was God really sending a sign? Had they all just witnessed a miracle?

After his parents died, John of Dunois was raised with the dauphin, and the pair remained friends for life.

chapter 7

"Fight for France!"

John of Dunois broke the stunned silence, ordering everyone down to the shore. His men jumped into action, loading every fishing boat tied to the bank and waiting for their important passengers. The regular troops could march back to Blois and wait for orders there.

This map shows the city of Orléans as it existed during the siege, along with the English forts surrounding it.

Joan refused to go. There were not enough boats for the soldiers who had marched upriver with her. They were cleansed and ready for holy battle, she said. They had confessed and fasted. They had all taken communion and prayed with her. Now Dunois wanted them to march all the way back to Blois without her?

Dunois pointed out that they could cross the river easily at the shallows in Blois. They would arrive only a few days later and bring all the supplies with them. Besides, all of Orléans was expecting her arrival. Joan reluctantly agreed to separate from her troops. They marched off into the night and Joan boarded a boat.

As the sun set, Joan and her companions sailed across the Loire with ease. A few hours later, Joan made a dramatic entrance into Orléans, through the French-controlled Burgundy Gate. Carrying her banner, she rode on a milk white horse, her armor glinting silver in the torchlight. The citizens of Orléans went wild. They pressed in at every side, wanting simply to touch this young woman who had come to save their city. Cheers rose in waves as the story of the miraculous weather change swept the crowd. Church bells pealed from every steeple. Hands reached to pat the white warhorse. Babies were held up to see the famous Maid.

Joan entered Orleans triumphantly, surrounded by cheering townspeople from all walks of life.

Suddenly, fire jumped from a torch to the corner of Joan's banner. Onlookers screamed. They began to stampede.

Joan deftly turned her enormous steed. She smothered the flames neatly against the city wall. She had her horse wheel again and resumed her

Jacques Boucher's house still stands in Orléans. It was built in the "half-timber" style common in the 1400s.

place in line. The Orleanians cheered all the louder. How could a mere girl be such a horsewoman, they wondered. She was as wonderful as all the rumors they'd heard!

By the far wall of town, Joan's party dismounted. The Count of Dunios introduced her to a middle-aged commoner, Jacques Boucher, who told Joan that she was welcome to stay in his house. It was a relief to walk inside, remove her armor, and sit on a bench. Joan refused a meal, though she had not eaten all day. Instead, she asked for wine and bread. As had become her habit, she added water to the wine. Then she dipped the bread into it and ate. She spent the night in a bed with the Boucher's nine-year-old daughter to guard her privacy.

Joan had ached to do battle for months. Now she was in Orléans sleeping in a cozy family home while her troops marched away toward Blois. Early the next morning, she snuck out to look over the city's battlements and learn its layout. At once, people began cheering and following her around. They reached out to touch her and got in her way.

Joan returned to the Bouchers' for her horse and a page or two. Together, they rode through the streets.

Once, Joan climbed a turret in the city wall. Seeing Englishmen patrolling the road beyond, she yelled at them, telling them to go away in God's name. Then she threatened to drive them out. One of them shouted insults about her and her troops. He said he would never surrender to a woman.

All day long, Joan paced the city. Later in the evening, her temper flared again. She leaned from the ramparts by the bridge of Orléans and yelled to the English. Once more, she demanded that they surrender.

They called her a cowherd and shouted that they would burn her alive if they ever got hold of her.

This illustration of the Siege of Orléans, created in 1484, shows the city, the Loire, and an English bastide.

With notched walls and watchtowers at each gate, walled cities were designed to resist attack.

Sunday passed. Dunois left town with a company of soldiers to meet the supplies heading from Blois. Monday and Tuesday, Joan paced about, bound by a promise not to attack anyone until Dunois returned. On Wednesday, he was back. Joan's men marched behind him, along with other French troops. To the joy of the city, they brought desperately needed supplies. Thousands of soldiers camped in the countryside around the Burgundy Gate. Dunois had thrilling news for Joan, too.

An English army, headed by John Fastolf was on its way to Orléans. Joan, tired of waiting and fearful of being tricked, demanded to be told the moment Fastolf arrived so she could get into her armor and lead her troops. Dunois promised, and Joan went to bed feeling secure.

A few hours later, her voices awakened her and she sprang from bed. The battle had begun while she rested! She demanded her horse, her armor, some clothes, and her banner all at once. Joan was furious. Why had no one told her? Her pages and squires ran around trying to follow her orders. At one point she was downstairs on horseback, ready to go, without her banner. It had to be handed to her through the bedroom window. Then she was off galloping through the streets to the Burgundy Gate.

Almost at once, Joan had to wheel her horse around a fallen French soldier. Another lay groaning in a puddle of blood in the road. A pair of soldiers limped past, half carrying a wounded comrade back toward the shelter of Orléans. Gasping, they told her that some territory had been won. Joan had never seen so many battle wounds before. She wanted to weep. Instead, she spurred her horse ahead.

Joan's bright armor, white banner, and pale horse made her visible above the bloody hand-to-hand battle.

"The Maid!" shouted a French soldier. "The Maid comes!" The cry spread through the ranks. Men who had been happy just to force the English off a ridge pressed harder. Their arrows flew with fresh force. They rushed to thrust their pikes into enemy bodies. Joan rode into the middle of the battle. Swords flashed around her. Men cried out, "The Maid rides!" One Englishman swung his ball and chain toward a Frenchman. It crunched through his skull.

Prayer before and after the battle gave Joan strength. Her voices urged her on while she gave others courage.

That soldier died, but another slashed a dagger across the Englishman's gut. Blood was everywhere among the screams and battle cries. Joan did not draw her weapon, but held her banner tall in the front lines. "Fight for France!" she shouted.

And they did, overwhelming the bastide the English had built to guard the old Roman road to Saint Loup. They fought to the last man, leaving no Englishmen to take shelter in the other bastides encircling Orléans. As dark fell, bodies littered the ground. A company of French stayed behind to hold the little fort in case any English arrived from other bastides. The rest rode back to Orléans.

They arrived in high spirits, bragging of their victory. They raved about the difference Joan had made. They'd been about to give up. The bravery of the Maid had inspired them to a level of courage and strength they'd never felt before. The dead were counted and the wounded tended to. Then it was time for wine, song, and celebration.

Joan wept inconsolably in the church. What had seemed a simple plan had led to terrible consequences. Between sobs she told the priest about the victims, French and English. They had not confessed before they died! That meant no priest had forgiven their sins. Who knew how long their souls would have to suffer for those sins before they could move on to heaven? They prayed together for those poor souls. Joan confessed her own sins and the priest served her communion. Comforted, she remained kneeling before the altar, praying long into the night.

The next day was Ascension Thursday, a holy day in the church. Joan declared that she would not start a battle or even put on her armor out of respect for this day. She could barely contain herself, though. Twice during the day, she had notes written demanding surrender. Her heralds carried them to the English. Against all rules of chivalry, the English took one of her heralds hostage. Joan dictated a third letter, offering to release some English prisoners in exchange for her herald. This time, she tied the letter to an arrow with a thread. Then she ordered an archer to shoot it into the enemy camp. The sound of English laughter and name-calling floated clearly back to Orléans.

Chivalry

In the Middle Ages, French knights were known as *chevaliers*, or horsemen. Over time, the word *chivalry* began to refer to a code of knightly behavior. Although details varied, a knight was generally expected to be courageous, honorable, loyal to the church, gracious to women, and to fight injustice wherever it lay. Many stories from this time praised the chivalrous deeds of famous knights.

8

Triumph in Orléans

On Friday, Joan took communion early and suited up in her armor. Her company of pages, squires, heralds, and guards prepared for battle. They marched toward the Burgundy Gate, where the governor of Orléans, Raoul de Gaucourt, blocked her way. He told her the captains had decided: There was to be no fighting that day. More reinforcements were on the way and she should wait.

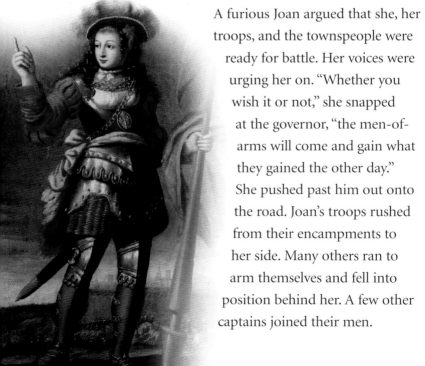

Although this 17th-century painting captures Joan's brave spirit, the feathered bonnet is an unlikely accessory.

A furious Joan argued that she, her troops, and the townspeople were ready for battle. Her voices were urging her on. "Whether you wish it or not," she snapped at the governor, "the men-of-arms will come and gain what they gained the other day." She pushed past him out onto the road. Joan's troops rushed from their encampments to her side. Many others ran to arm themselves and fell into position behind her. A few other captains joined their men.

The modern city of Orléans is dominated by its cathedral. In the foreground is the bridge where Joan battled the English.

They marched up the north bank of the river without contest. Halfway across the Loire the English had built a little fort on a long, skinny island, the Île-aux-Toiles. Joan and the captains who had scrambled into place beside her stared across the water. They decided to attack. The soldiers made a bridge by linking boats together and laying boards across them. They marched across this pontoon bridge to one end of the island and prepared to attack.

No one came out to fight. The English had already abandoned the little fort! They had retreated the length of the Île-aux-Toiles and waded to the south bank where the big bastide of Augustins stood. This fort was one of the biggest the English had built around Orléans.

This bastide was far too large for Joan's troops to take alone. Even with the extra men, they would be outnumbered.

The dramatic image of Joan of Arc charging into battle has inspired many paintings. This one is from the early 1900s.

The soldiers shifted uneasily. Retreat is a dangerous maneuver. Troops are vulnerable to attack from all sides. They expected the order to retreat, so they formed up to leave the island, Joan guarding the rear.

The English troops saw this and began pouring out of the bastide of Augustins. The front lines waded over to the island through the shallows. They began running after the retreating French, their swords at the ready.

Joan called a halt and charged straight at the English. Her captains and troops turned in surprise and scrambled to follow. They poured across the island, whooping and screaming. They had the advantage, and they knew it. More importantly, they had the Maid.

Given time, the English would have set up defensive lines. They would have set a row of pikes into the ground, aimed at their attackers. They would have had archers ready in formation. Instead they fought in confusion, hand to hand. The French were fewer in number than the English but they were wild to win.

By sheer force, they drove the English back to Augustins. Then, incredibly, they surrounded that fort and took Augustins, too. The English troops who could save themselves retreated to a nearby bastide called Tourelles at the southern end of the bridge across the Loire.

Joan spent the night in the Augustins fort, along with the French captains and their men. The citizens of Orléans sent them boatloads of fresh food and wine. The men celebrated. Joan prayed. But the lords and captains held a meeting. Joan had managed to do in days what they had not accomplished in seven months. She had not come up through the military ranks. She was not from the nobility, either. They didn't know what she was planning for the next day's actions. Once again, they made a plan without her.

The men sent word to Joan. They were outnumbered by the English and Orléans was in no real danger of starving now.

Feather plumes made officers more visible in battle. Here, a captain stands beside one of the dauphin's knights.

Perhaps it would be better to stay where they were and wait for reinforcements from the king.

Joan paid no attention to them. She ordered her men to an early mass in the morning, then launched an attack on the fortress of Tourelles. Augustins was big, but Tourelles was critical. It guarded the only bridge across the Loire for miles.

The fighting was fierce. Troops stormed the fort under their shields while the English dropped stones and shot arrows down into their ranks. Frenchmen catapaulted stones into the fort. Joan rushed ahead to put the first ladder up to the wall. She made it halfway up before an Englishman on top heaved the ladder away. Again and again, the French raised ladders to mount the walls. They were repelled with swords and clubs. The men hacked and slashed, fought and fell. When they saw the Maid's banner, they rose and fought again.

While Joan climbs a ladder at Tourelles, defenders fire arrows from above. The artist has added a skirt to her armor.

Around midday, Joan was shot with an arrow. As she had predicted, it drove into her body above her breast. She wept in pain and surprise. Her voices hadn't told her how much it would hurt. She was carried back to the safety of Augustins. A soldier offered to say a healing charm over the wound as she lay on the ground. Joan refused, saying she would rather die than deal in ungodly magic. Another soldier suggested that he dress the wound with olive oil and bacon fat and plug it with cotton. Joan agreed, then reached up and pulled the arrow out of her own flesh. Blood gushed out before the wound was covered. Then she had to rest.

Within a few hours, she was back in the thick of battle. The fighting raged on all afternoon. Joan ordered her troops to fill a barge with tar and wood and tie it under the first arch of the bridge. When they set it on fire, the flames and churning black smoke filled the bastide.

The English fought as if they were cornered; the French, as if inspired. By late day all were exhausted. Dunois approached Joan cautiously. He told her he was going to call the battle off. She told him to call a break instead. The men needed food and drink and a moment's breather. She needed to pray. Joan rode her horse into a vineyard near the troops. She headed back in a quarter hour.

A squire who was carrying her banner stepped into a ditch. The painting of Jesus and Mary almost hit the dirt. Joan leaped and grabbed the banner to save it. That made it flap so violently that

A priest places the Eucharist on Joan's tongue. Today, Catholics can also choose to be handed the wafer by their priest.

all of her troops assumed it was a signal. They rushed together, rallied, and stormed the bastide with renewed strength. Within a few hours it was over. They had taken Tourelles and, with it, the bridge across the Loire.

Wild parties and rejoicing filled the night. Joan grieved, instead. Frenchmen had died horribly in the bloodfest of the day. Hundreds of English lives had been lost, too. William Gladsdale, a famous English general, had fallen off the bridge in his armor and drowned, as had many of his countrymen. Jesus had loved all of them, and now they were dead.

Sunday morning dawned clear and fair. When the French looked over the walls of Orléans they saw that all the surviving English soldiers had gathered in battle formation near the city. The rules of chivalry demanded that there be no fighting on the Sabbath. But the French troops were already suiting up, eager to finish the fight. Joan raced to get ready. She told her army to fan out in battle formation, facing the English. They could only defend themselves, she said. They could not start a fight.

Once the men were lined up, they had to stare right into the English faces only feet away. Neither side moved.

No one wanted to dishonor his country by breaking the code of chivalry. Then, because it was Sunday, Joan had her priests give communion in the space between the armies. In absolute silence the English watched the French receive the Eucharist. After an hour and a half, the English simply turned and left. They cleared out their bastides and marched away toward English-controlled Paris.

Orléans was free! May 8, 1429, was one of the strangest mornings in any war, won decisively by a test of wills. Joan was not about to celebrate. She had known she would triumph at Orléans. Now she had a king to crown.

This painting depicts Joan entering Orléans on the night of May 8, 1429, just after the English had been driven out for good.

9

The Maid Fights On

Word of Joan's triumph reached the dauphin in
Chinon through a series of breathless messengers.
Young Charles sent out a letter to be read in every loyal
French town, celebrating the defeat of the English at Orléans.

It was getting warm in France so the dauphin moved to Loches, his favorite summer residence, 10 miles from Chinon on the Indre River. With him came

Angels accompany Joan
as she rides up to Chinon
to announce her victory in
Orléans to the dauphin.

a large company made up of friends, advisers, pages, cooks, and almost everyone else in his court. They all settled in for a long, relaxing stay.

Meanwhile, the good news about Orléans spread across the country. Many Burgundians felt a secret surge of patriotism and longing for a free France. They began to mutter about overthrowing their English masters.

Although the castle at Loches was a luxurious getaway for the dauphin, many sections have now fallen into ruin.

Joan and the Count of Dunois hurried their armies to Loches and demanded to speak with the dauphin. Joan had already sent word that she wanted Charles to go to Reims immediately. Reims was deep in English territory, but it was vital that Charles be anointed in the city's cathedral, where French kings were traditionally crowned.

The dauphin had never been very excited about becoming king. He liked being comfortable and surrounded by friends. Joan wanted to push him into more danger—and responsibility—than he'd ever wanted. The dauphin kept Joan and her enormous army waiting for two weeks while he and his advisors decided what to do.

This painting shows the castle at Loches in all its glory, as Joan meets with the reluctant dauphin in the courtyard.

The dauphin's friends told him not to risk the trip to Reims, especially since they had just arrived in Loches. What if Joan's win at Orléans was a fluke? A loss now would demoralize the entire country again and make the dauphin look foolish. Instead of going with Joan now, they suggested, Charles should let her go on ahead and recapture a few cities on the way to Reims. Once he saw how the battles were going, the dauphin could follow the cleared path to his coronation. That might take a long time, of course. Until then, the advisors slyly suggested, they could all stay in beautiful Loches.

Joan was wildly impatient by the time the dauphin finally admitted her to his court on May 13. She carried her banner in with her, a German observer reported. She "bowed as deeply as she could before him, and the king promptly made her rise. From the joy he expressed, one would have thought that he might have hugged her."

Joan looked around at the smug circle of advisors and demanded to speak with him alone. He had to move, she told him, and now. Her troops were feeling invincible, and more volunteers were arriving every day to fight with her for France. Joan told the dauphin that wherever they marched to battle now, they would win. Having a French king on the throne would guarantee it. Besides, the voices were telling Joan she had less than a year left.

The dauphin began to explain his alternate plan. Joan threw herself onto her knees and threw her arms around his legs to show her devotion—and to beg for quick, definitive action. "Do not hold a council meeting for such a long time," she demanded, "but come to Reims to receive a worthy crown!"

On May 24, Joan left Loches to clear the dauphin's path, as he had decided. She first stopped to persuade her old friend the Duke of Alençon to come fight with her. He was willing, but his wife argued against it. "Lady," Joan said, "have no fear; I shall bring him back to you in good health and in better shape than he is now!"

Joan's frustration can be plainly seen, as she pleads with the dauphin in this 19th-century portrait.

Finally, in early June, with almost 2,000 men assembled behind her, Joan left on her Loire campaign. Her

Bridge battles were a common part of the conflict between France and England, as shown in this medieval illustration.

object was to recapture a series of towns along the Loire River. These towns had only recently been captured by the English, and the English and Burgundian troops were spread thin in the area. Alençon, an old military man, was in charge of Joan's army. The Count of Dunois and his companion, Florent d'Illiers, joined them along the way, commanding another 2,000 men. The first battle was held at the English-held town of Jargeau.

The three commanders hesitated before battle. We are badly outnumbered, they told Joan. She insisted they attack at once, riding into battle herself. After fierce fighting, they took the suburbs up to the Jargeau wall. Early the next morning, Alençon again asked Joan to reconsider.

Her answer stuck in his mind. "Are you afraid, gentle duke?" she said. "Do you not know that I promised your wife to bring you back safe and sound?"

Later that morning, as they fought side by side, Joan shouted at Alençon to move. She said he would be struck by a stone hurled over the city wall. Alençon wasn't sure whether to believe her, but he moved anyway. Another man took his place. Moments later, a boulder hurled by a catapault slammed into Alençon's replacement, killing him on impact.

Later in the battle, Joan leaned a siege ladder against the wall. She began to climb, but was hit on the head by a boulder dropped from above.

The rock hit her helmet and split in two. Joan fell backward, clinging to the ladder. She hit the ground in full armor. Around her, soldiers froze. Joan just laughed and struggled back to her feet. She took a breath and shouted, "Up, up my friends! Our Lord has condemned the English.

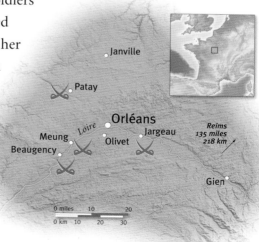

This map shows the area where Joan conducted her Loire campaign. Major battles are marked with sword symbols.

While Joan's pages helped her into her heavy armor before a battle, her squires dressed and readied her horses.

At this very hour they are ours; take courage!" The city was taken before nightfall.

Joan and Alençon left enough men to hold the city, then marched to Orléans to plan their next move. The following day, they took the city of Meung and an all-important bridge over the Loire. Joan sent half of her troops on ahead to Beaugency, a town guarding another bridge further up the Loire.

The city fathers of Beaugency did not want their town to be in the middle of the immense battle that was brewing. They surrendered without a fight. The English military retreated into the castle guarding the bridge.

Joan's army had grown enormously, but so had the English armies before them. Joan's old enemy, the English commander John Fastolf, was hurrying his forces across the countryside toward her armies. English commanders everywhere in Europe were on the move. They had to stop the Maid before she united all of France!

On June 16, Fastolf arrived at Janville, 30 miles (48 km) northeast of Beaugency. He brought 5,000 relief troops for the English. Joan's forces swelled by 2,000 that same day when the dauphin's commander, Arthur de Richemont, reported for duty. The battle was going to be as big as the dreadful day at Agincourt when the English had made the French look so helpless. The English could taste a repeat success, but Joan had control of both bridges over the Loire.

The English divisions could not contact each other across the river and mistakes left whole armies of English and Burgundian troops without cover or food. Some surrendered while others strengthened their defenses. Finally, in the evening, the French and English armies met face-to-face. Joan declared that the French would not fight until the next day.

The next morning the English were gone! Thousands of troops had retreated in silence through the woods. The French troops gave chase, led by 70 trackers. For miles, they marched through the woods, searching for any sign of a passing army. As it turned out, both groups were hustling toward the same place: the town of Patay. Incredibly, they never caught sight of each other.

On June 18, the English armies turned and began setting up their defenses.

This engraving shows the French scouts searching through deep forests for the fleeing English army.

They planned to set spikes, dig ditches, and prepare for a grand stand. The French trackers approached at dawn, not knowing how close they were. The English troops awoke in silence, unaware of the danger lurking.

Suddenly a buck with huge antlers leaped through the English lines. The soldiers instinctively gave chase, each wanting to claim the animal for himself. Yelling and shouting, they ran right into the forward guard of the French army.

One old legend foretold that a maiden's horse would trample the backs of bowmen. Joan seemed to fulfill this prophecy.

The startled French ignored the buck, but chased the English back into their camp. The English held only shovels, pillows, or breakfast sausages. The French held swords, bows, and maces. The English hadn't gotten dressed yet. The French wore full suits of armor. The huge battle that followed was as one-sided and humiliating as the battle of Agincourt—only this time the French won.

Just three French soldiers died in battle at Patay. By their own count, the English and Burgundian forces lost

2,000 men. Other sources say it was closer to 4,000. Fastolf scuttled away under a white flag of surrender.

Hearing about this fantastic victory, the dauphin traveled to the town of Gien, which lay on the way to Reims. Joan met him there two days later, on June 25, ready to march onward. As usual, Charles's advisors talked him into waiting. Frustrated, Joan and her troops took positions outside of town. The royal party feared that she was going to attack or abandon them in response to their stalling. They quickly packed for Reims.

Joan's army was 10,000 strong now, with more soldiers arriving by the hour. They were willing to fight without pay, just so they could be at Joan's side. Even with the reluctant dauphin along, this immense army easily mowed through Auxerre on July 3, Troyes on July 9, and Châlons-sur-Marne on July 14. On July 16, they reached Reims. The English sympathizers in the city surrendered immediately. The dauphin, his advisors, and Joan staged a triumphal entry before cheering crowds. "Noël! Noël! Noël!" they cried, repeating the age-old French welcome for an uncrowned king.

Joan, shown inaccurately with long hair and a dress, convinces the dauphin to go to Reims.

10

Crowning the King

Charles arrived in Reims on a Saturday. Joan knew it was critically important to crown the new French king according to ancient traditions, and coronations were traditionally held on Sundays. Reims townspeople had been generous in their welcome—Joan didn't want to ask them to feed and house an army of 12,000 for an extra week, too. Such a large number of soldiers deep in the Duke of Burgundy's territory could trigger another major battle, especially when the English and Burgundians were so opposed to the coronation.

They were right to be uneasy about it. Being a king in the Middle Ages meant much more than

Like many French cathedrals built after 1200, the one at Reims has a round stained-glass "rose window."

wearing a crown. It was a holy sacrament. In the eyes of believers, the sacrament of baptism made a baby into member of the church. The sacrament of marriage bound two people together forever. The sacrament of ordination changed an ordinary man into a priest. Similarly, the anointing of a king made a normal man into something else entirely. Each sacrament took place within a grand formal ceremony, carried out with precision.

Anointing

Many religions feature some form of anoninting ceremony, in which a person is rubbed with oil or a similar substance, symbolizing the transfer of a holy spirit or power. When a Catholic king was anointed, it indicated that he had been given the divine right to rule. Above, Clovis I is anointed by the bishop of Reims.

The English Henry VI had been named King of France when he was still a baby, but he had not been anointed with oil from the *sainte ampoule*. That holy vial of oil was said to have been used around 496, during the baptism of Clovis I, the man the French consider their first king. Legend said that angels had brought it down from heaven for him. Since then it had been kept safe at the abbey in Reims. It was only taken out for coronations.

ABBEY

An abbey is a religious campus where monks or nuns live and worship, apart from the world.

Comment ceulx de reims ouurirent

Charles VII was crowned in robes trimmed with ermine fur. An ermine is a kind of weasel that turns white in winter.

On Saturday night, the dauphin quietly entered the archbishop's palace in Reims. He held vigil there all night, praying for the guidance, strength, and wisdom a king would need. Early in the morning of July 17, four knights in full armor rode on horseback through the town to the abbey. These Guardians of the Holy Vial waited until the abbot brought his treasure out to them.

In formation, the four guardians escorted the abbot and the *sainte ampoule* back toward the cathedral under a golden canopy. They joined the procession of bishops and other churchmen who surrounded the dauphin. He was humbly dressed in shoes and a simple, knee-length shirt. Hundreds of worshippers inside the cathedral cheered as the group moved toward the altar, the horses' hooves clattering on the marble floor. Joan waited for them in the front, her battle standard held high. At the top of a short flight of stairs, a throne waited for the dauphin.

The dauphin swore lifelong loyalty to his kingdom, the country, and its people. Next, monks and priests from the abbey sang an ancient chant. The archbishop blessed all the symbols of the king's power: the crown, the golden spurs, the scepter, and a second scepter called the Hand of Justice. After that, the king lay flat on the floor, his arms stretched toward the altar. Beside him, the archbishop lay down, too.

Reciting a long prayer to all the saints, the archbishop knelt and opened the holy vial. He dipped a long pin inside to touch the few precious drops left inside, then mixed them with newly blessed oil. With this, he anointed the king's head, chest, shoulders, elbows, and wrists.

The Hand of Justice symbolized the absolute power of the French king. His word was law.

The dauphin rose and put on a tunic and a coat of finest silk. He was anointed on his hands before pulling on a pair of gloves. The ring that would bind him forever to his people was slipped on his finger over the glove. The crown was lowered onto his head. As he walked up the steps to the throne, he turned to face his subjects. Joan moved up to stand beside him. To her, this seemed perfectly natural. After all,

she had been the one to make sure Charles was crowned. Nevertheless, many people were startled, as they realized that Joan had broken tradition. Then the blare of dozens of trumpets filled the cathedral. The crowd cheered "Noël" again, but now to their rightful king.

One by one, the church leaders knelt before him to swear loyalty. After that, the noblemen knelt in order to pledge their lives to the new King Charles VII. Then Joan slipped into line. She knelt and began to sob with relief. She leaned forward to clasp her arms around the knees of the newly consecrated king.

Joan broke the rules when she stood at the altar during Charles's coronation. The area was reserved for priests.

"Gentle king," she said, "now is executed the will of God who wished the siege of Orléans should be lifted, and that you should be brought to the city of Reims to receive your holy consecration, thus showing you are a true king, and he to whom the kingdom of France should belong."

Joan made sure she was at the king's side throughout the week-long festivities that followed. She was alive with energy, excitement, and inspiration, but she didn't make any friends.

The courtiers had never liked her. Now some clerics turned against her, too. Bishops, friars, priests, and others who had devoted their entire lives to the Roman Catholic Church envied the voices that came easily to Joan. It shook their faith, and gave Joan more credibility than they had. Some of them began to spread rumors, questioning her honesty.

Most discouraging for Joan, the new king's coronation hadn't changed him one bit. He still depended on his friends' advice too much. He still preferred delay and negotiation to decisive action.

Today, a statue of Joan of Arc stands in Reims cathedral, along with a replica of her battle flag.

Joan knew they had to take advantage of the progress the army had made, and soon. She dictated a letter to the Duke of Burgundy, offering peace but threatening military action if he did not pledge loyalty to the new king. Joan had learned to make the letters of her name. She proudly signed this letter and handed it to her messenger.

The Duke of Burgundy ignored her note. He was already negotiating a secret deal with her king.

This is one of three surviving examples of Joan's signature. She always signed her name as *Jehanne*, with no last name.

chapter **11**

On to Paris!

Joan nagged at Charles, demanding that they march on Paris. If they conquered Paris, all of France would be his. Her troops were battle-ready, gathered around Reims. Everyone expected the new king to take control. Summer was the best time to move through the country. All of Joan's reasons were good ones. Her only strategy was to put the obvious truth before him. It was time to attack Paris.

She did not know that Charles was negotiating a deal with the Duke of Burgundy under which he promised not to attack Paris for 15 days. At the end of that period, the Duke of Burgundy promised to turn the city over to the king.

While Joan urged immediate attack, the new king spent four full days sending messengers to and from Paris, getting the wording right on his treaty. Joan had been around French nobility for a year now. She knew the court was full of secrets and lies.

It took single-minded focus, firey determination, and uncompromising faith to fight for a free France.

Charles told Joan they were going to march soon, but he made no move to begin preparations. Joan was smart enough to wonder what was going on. She began to worry about treachery from her enemies in Charles's court.

Of course, the hostility of the court paled in comparison to the wrath of Joan's English and Burgundian enemies.

The Duke of Burgundy founded an order promoting chivalry. Despite this, he wasn't a very trustworthy negotiator.

They wanted her dead, for many reasons. She had masterminded the capture of city after city from the English. Her troops had slaughtered Burgundian armies at the Battle of Patay. Worse, her inspiration seemed to be turning the tide of the long war. It now seemed France might drive England out. Anyone who had fought against France would be punished.

Paris, the center of Burgundian power, was the largest city in medieval Europe. The University of Paris was a hub of learning in the Middle Ages. The school had always focused on classics, history, and the church, but now it encouraged the growth of new ideas. Change was in the air there, and Joan seemed to stand for the old ways.

The University of Paris

In the 12th century, there was an increasing demand for educated clerics. To help meet this need, a group of Parisian scholars founded the Universitas: a club of professors and students who banded together to study. Later, this club was given its own rooms by the church, and it evolved into the University of Paris, one of the models for our modern universities.

She had crowned a French king with traditional powers. He had the "divine right" to insist on complete loyalty from his subjects. People at the university preferred the idea of being ruled by an English king. They reasoned that a king stretched thin by ruling two countries wouldn't have time to worry about what was discussed in schools or how people spoke about their ruler.

Another idea supported in the university was a general council that would supervise the pope. This would limit the power of the pope's courts to punish scholars for their new ways of thinking. Joan's victories and her visions had reminded people of the incredible power of simple faith and unquestioning obedience to the church.

The members of the university saw Joan as a threat to their radical ideas. But, at the same time, Joan seemed to have some radical ideas of her own. After all, she had earned her success in a world ruled by men. During the Middle Ages, all military soldiers and leaders were men. All church leaders were men. All professors were men. All doctors, judges, bankers, and butchers were men. Women were not even allowed to wear men's clothes. The image of a teenage girl wearing real battle armor and commanding thousands of men threatened the stability of their society. Whether she represented the old ways or the new, many people wished her gone.

Joan knew she was relatively safe with Charles VII, though she wished he'd be more decisive. After stalling for a week, the king took another to travel to nearby villages. An old tradition said that the touch of a new king's hands, recently anointed with holy oil, would cure the sick. People, old and young, waited patiently for hours, hoping for a royal miracle. Joan did not wait patiently.

Dating from around 1600, this map of Paris shows the city's impressive medieval fortifications.

Based on a medieval tapestry, this drawing shows Charles VII in ceremonial armor, riding atop an equally armored horse.

Finally, the king agreed to move on Paris. It was only 90 miles away, but it took the armies 36 days to get there. Charles insisted on stopping in every town to greet his subjects. When battles were likely, he and his court waited comfortably in friendly castles.

The Duke of Burgundy had no intention of honoring his treaty with Charles VII, even for a few days. While the French king dawdled across the countryside, the Duke of Burgundy raised new armies to protect Paris. Stone masons reinforced the city walls. Blacksmiths forged new swords. Archers made hundreds of new sharp-tipped arrows. They knew a battle was coming.

Joan's army was falling apart. Her volunteers drifted off, returning to their farms in time for harvest. The captains could see who was in charge—and it wasn't Joan anymore. Messengers began to lose her orders, or show them to her enemies. To try to maintain some control, Joan devised a code. If she drew a circle below her signature with a cross inside, her friends knew she meant just the opposite of what the letter said. She learned at last to guard her words and be careful whom she trusted.

As they got closer to Paris, the Duke of Bedford, the English commander, sent a letter challenging Charles to fight. Dated August 7, it sneered that Charles relied "upon the assistance of the superstitious and reprobate, and even of that deranged and infamous woman who goes about in men's clothes and is of dissolute conduct."

Joan was still wearing men's clothes for comfort and safety in the field. Living with the troops, hardly anyone could believe she wasn't involved with a man yet. At the very least, they figured she was drinking with the soldiers.

In fact, Joan was struggling to lead. Since the king wasn't about to order a battle, Joan and her forces moved in to survey the Parisian defenses at close range. With only 500 men, there was little hope they could take the city. To get close enough to study the wall, Joan's troops needed to cross the moat. As her men shoveled dirt into the broad ditch, Joan rode back and forth with her banner, urging them on.

An arrow from an enemy crossbow slammed into her thigh and she fell. She was quickly carried off the field. Another general ordered the withdrawal

Joan's attack of Paris was unsuccessful. Her soldiers carry the wooden shields common in the 1400s.

In a time with no anesthesia or antibiotics, operations on wounded soldiers were very often fatal.

of all her troops. Unbeknownst to her, the Duke of Burgundy and King Charles were busily negotiating yet another treaty. Joan was plainly getting in the way. Now she was out of action with a deep muscle wound.

Joan spent most of the late fall recuperating at court. She prayed for hours, speaking with her priest. She listened to her voices, too. Now they were telling her she would be taken prisoner before June 21, Midsummer's Day. Joan kept urging the king to press on to Paris.

On December 29, 1429, Charles VII officially made her a noblewoman of the kingdom of France. Her family was given the name du Lis, meaning "of the Lily." Joan, now Lady du Lis, was deeply flattered. This title gave her the right to a coat of arms showing the fleur de lis. She could wear it into battle and use it to identify any possessions. She could raise her own funds and command her own army. In France, positions of nobility were passed through the men of the family. Charles made an exception for Joan's relatives.

At this point, Joan made a sophisticated move worthy of an experienced member of court. She talked the king into granting her town, Domrémy, and the nearby safehold of Greux, tax-free status forever. No longer would the farmers, shoemakers, and smiths have to set aside part of their produce for the king each year. That agreement stood until the French Revolution, hundreds of years later.

Joan slowly discovered that the king wasn't just being nice to her. He was pushing her further away. Because Joan now was a noblewoman in her own right, he did not need to provide her with housing, food, or clothing. He did not have to provide for her squires, pages, and brothers anymore. She was on her own to feed and stable her horses, too. Most nobles had land they could use to generate income. Joan had none. Luckily, she did have rich friends happy to support her in her mission. But now Joan could only command her own troops, not those of the king.

With this letter, Charles VII assigned Joan her coat of arms: a sword supporting a crown, flanked by a pair of fleur de lis.

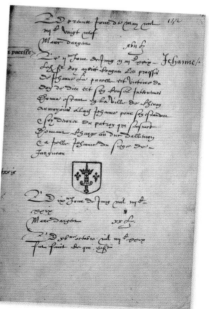

Once her leg had recovered, Joan demanded that the king send her into battle again. She had secured funds for only one page, her horses, and a small band of men, but she longed to accomplish something before her battle days were

In the ceremony of baptism, a priest anoints a baby with holy water and oil. The baby then becomes a member of the church.

over. She ended up leaving without King Charles's blessing.

She visited friendly cities first: Melun and Lagny. Then she fought a band of Burgundians led by the notorious highwayman Franquet d'Arras. She delivered d'Arras to the courts. After 15 days in court, he was pronounced guilty and sentenced to death as a murderer, a thief, and a traitor.

One day, as Joan rode through Lagny, a family begged her to help their newborn baby. He was deathly ill, his body limp and discolored, but he had not yet been baptized. Medieval priests taught that people—even babies—who died without being a member of the church spent eternity in hell. This baby couldn't be baptized because no one was sure he was alive. Joan stepped into the small home and stared at the baby. She later said he was "as black as my coat of mail." She fell to her knees and prayed to Mary in heaven. Though he had lain as if dead for three days, the infant suddenly awoke and yawned three times. He was baptized and died. Then he was buried in holy ground, to the tears and relief of his family. As always, word of Joan's newest miracle spread throughout the country.

COURSER

A courser was a light, fast, strong war horse used for intense battle.

On May 14, the town of Compiègne invited her to a reception. Several other dignitaries were there, each with their own small armies. The Burgundians attacked nearby and the combined armies were forced in a bloody battle back to Soissens. From all around, volunteers loyal to the English hurried to fight against the famous Joan. On May 23, 1430, her forces began to back down towards the walled city of Compiègne, where they could take shelter.

Joan stayed behind to guard their rear. Wearing a gold doublet over her silvery armor, riding a light gray courser, and carrying her battle flag, she rode back and forth, urging her men on. By dozens, by tens, and then by twos, her soldiers scuttled to safety through the city gate.

The grid of planks shown here is a portcullis. Dropping one in front of a gate provided an extra measure of defense.

Without warning, the portcullis slammed down. The last man to enter barely got inside. Joan did not. Neither did her page, Jean, or her brother, Pierre. Joan pulled her horse to a halt before the gate. Had someone meant to let her in and misjudged the timing? Or had one of Joan's enemies finally trapped her? To this day, no one knows.

chapter 12

Prisoner of England

Joan froze, facing a line of archers, each aiming an arrow at her heart. Her horse snorted and pranced in place. She prayed only for a moment before the nearest archer handed his crossbow to a fellow soldier. He stepped quickly forward and grabbed the horse's reins to steady him. Then the soldier reached up, grasped Joan's golden tunic, and pulled her to the ground.

Joan lay where she had fallen. Any movement might have triggered an attack from the mob of troops gathered around her. The men hooted and cheered. Rude insults flew from all directions. So did death threats.

In the Middle Ages, soldiers were careful not to hurt important prisoners. Alive, they could be held for ransom.

These men finally had the Maid of Orléans trapped and helpless, and it took bellowed orders from the officers to keep them from tearing her to pieces. Finally, a captain pushed his way through to her and ordered the others back. He assumed that a high-value hostage like Joan could be exchanged for a huge ransom. This was the way many armies supported themselves during the Middle Ages. Joan would have to be kept in a safe place while negotiations went on for her release.

Joan now belonged to John of Luxembourg, who owned the land where she'd been captured. Luxembourg was a loyal friend of his ruler, the Duke of Burgundy, and

Joan's fateful capture at Compiègne is commemorated in a stained-glass window in the city's cathedral.

he also received monthly payments from the English. He took Joan home to his castle at Beaulieu to wait for ransom offers, along with her page and brother.

The Duke of Bedford wanted her. He'd been in charge of the military takeover of France, and Joan's ability to inspire the French had cost him dearly. The University of Paris wanted her. They stood for the Roman Catholic Church, and Joan was a holy figure completely out of their control.

King Charles VII wanted her—or at least he should have. Joan had gotten him crowned. She had rallied his people. The least he could do was set her free. But Charles preferred comfort to conflict. He relied on his advisors to

Witches

There have been many defintions of the word *witch* at different places and times. In medieval Europe, a witch was a woman who had made a pact with the devil in order to gain magical powers. Of course, such women did not exist, but from 1450 to 1700, fear of witches swept the continent, and tens of thousands of innocent women were put to death.

do his thinking for him. They were happy to have Joan locked up where she couldn't influence their king. They told him to wait and see what happened.

French people throughout the land marched and lit candles, demanding the release of the Maid. They prayed for her in great cathedrals and in humble shrines. Their children went to sleep with stories of Joan's holiness in their minds. People told of clouds of white butterflies drawn to her banner. The Maid seemed like a living saint, and they wanted her to be freed from her imprisonment.

English sympathizers told tales of a French sorceress instead. They called Joan a simple village girl, a clever witch, a devil worshipper, and a camp follower.

Within three days, Pierre Cauchon, bishop of Beauvais, offered to ransom Joan for 10,000 ecus, a small fortune. Cauchon was a Burgundian, loyal to the University of Paris where he had once worked. He also had a personal grudge against Joan. When her French army captured the English-controlled town where he was bishop, he'd lost his job—and his power over a huge congregation. Now he worked as a counselor to the Duke of Bedford.

Luxembourg did not turn Joan over to Cauchon. Instead he kept her as a prisoner and waited for more offers. Once, when Joan heard a rumor that she and her companions were going to be moved to another holding place, she tried to escape. She locked her guard in a room and set off to free her brother. Unfortunately, she was caught, and her guards were increased.

In the end, John of Luxembourg really did move his prisoner to a new holding place: the castle of Beaurevoir, far to the north. There, Joan was greeted by her keeper's aunt, Joan of Luxembourg, who had insisted on meeting the famous Maid of Orléans. This wealthy, powerful woman was startled by the

The Duke of Bedford was the brother of Henry V. The English gave him control over France, confident of his loyalty.

teenager's appearance. Unlike other women of the times, who let their hair grow as long as they lived, the Maid had chopped her hair off like a boy's. She dressed as a boy, too. And she was tiny. Joan of Arc often fasted and never ate a hearty meal. She picked at her food at banquets. Beyond that, she survived on no more than a few bites of bread dipped into wine. Though she was about 18 years old at the time of her capture, she looked much younger.

Joan of Luxembourg wanted to mother Joan, to nourish her and protect her. So did two other women at Beaurevoir. They, too, were named Joan: Joan of Bar and Joan of Bethune. These three Joans befriended their little prisoner, often visiting her quarters in the basement of one of the castle's towers. Joan of Arc later testified that "the lady of Luxembourg asked my lord of Luxembourg that I not be

Joan rode like a man on her way to prison. Most medieval women rode sidesaddle, with both legs on the same side.

delivered to the English." They all knew that would mean certain death.

Perhaps because of his aunt's cautions, Luxembourg held Joan, her brother, and her page for months. He might also have been waiting for an offer from the king of France.

Six months after her capture, Joan heard that she would be turned over to Bishop Cauchon. Luxembourg felt he had no choice. No one else had made an offer for the Maid.

Desperate, Joan climbed the stairs to the top of the tower. She looked over the edge. Sixty feet down was a dry moat. Could she survive the fall and escape? It was a terrible risk. Suicide was absolutely forbidden by the church and guaranteed an eternity in hell. Joan prayed. She listened to her voices. No, they said, but Joan jumped anyway.

She landed flat on the soft ground, stunned and badly bruised, but alive. She was in no shape to run for freedom, so Luxembourg's men gently carried her inside. Joan lay in bed, unable to eat or drink for two days. She often saw and talked with the saints and the archangel Michael. They hovered by her, declaring their love and wishing her strength to face what she had to do. They reassured her that she would be delivered soon. Joan began to heal, though she wept whenever her wondrous visions ended.

Finally, Cauchon arrived with 50 men-at-arms to move Joan to Rouen. They shifted her from castle to castle along the way, showing off their prize, always in leg irons and

Joan's conditions at Rouen were not nearly as pleasant as those she enjoyed as the captive of Jean de Luxembourg.

her boy's clothing. Rouen was in Normandy, a part of coastal France that had been loyal to England for 12 years. The young king of England was there. So were his counselors. They could watch as Cauchon brought their enemy down. Paris was the center of the church in France, but too many French sympathizers lived nearby. Rouen was a politically safe place to try Joan for heresy. Bishop Cauchon could hold an ecclesiastical trial there, with himself as judge.

At Rouen, Joan was treated as a despised prisoner, not a guest. She was locked in a small cell in the tower of the castle. She had heavy chains locked on her feet. Another chain connected her to a huge block of wood. An entire company of soldiers was ordered to guard her. Five of them were in the cell at all times. They harassed her verbally and threatened her, too. They slept with her in the cell. This made it hard for Joan to clear her mind enough to hear her voices. It also made it hard to keep herself from being molested.

Joan stayed in men's clothes. She was still the Maid, and had promised herself to God. "I do not dare take off these leggings, or wear them if they are not tightly laced," she told Cauchon. She had to scream for protection several times. Cauchon scolded her attackers, but gently. Since she was being tried for breaking church rules, Joan argued that she should be kept in an ecclesiastical prison. The church kept their women prisoners in monasteries with nuns as guards. That would be far safer—but it would make it harder for Cauchon to bring visitors by to see his famous captive.

There were other irregularities in this trial. Though she was a high-value prisoner of war, the English treated her like a common criminal. She would be tried by the church, but England was going to pay for the trial. Bishop Cauchon had no authority in Rouen. Technically, he could only be a judge where he was a bishop—in Beauvais, a town now held by the French. The English authorities swept all these complications aside. They wanted Joan dead.

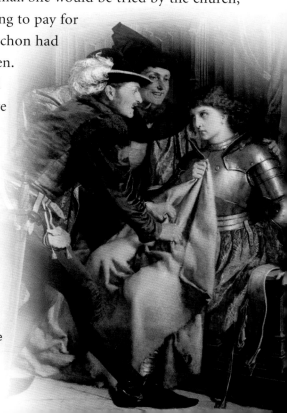

Some of Joan's guards were rude and threatening. Despite this illustration, Joan still wore men's clothes for protection.

13

Trial by Fire

Cauchon gathered 60 churchmen to preside over this mock trial. One pointed out that Joan had already been examined by the church, just before she marched on Orléans. She was proven innocent then—and still would be now. That priest was sent home. Another objected to the irregularities in the trial. He, too, was sent away. A third priest wanted nothing to do with the sham and refused to serve.

This trial was an inquisition, a formal inquiry into whether the church laws had been broken. Cauchon wanted the pope's Grand Inquisitor of the Faith and of Heretical

Error to preside with him, but he was busy in Rome. Instead, Jean le Maître, the sub-inquisitor arrived. He was reluctant to serve until the English threatened him. Even then, he only showed up at court occasionally.

The Cardinal of Winchester was one of many clerics who questioned Joan of Arc at Rouen. Cardinals could be recognized by their red robes.

A friend of Bishop Cauchon's, Jean d'Estivet was named prosecutor. Joan would have no defense lawyer or advisor. She could call no witnesses. She was assumed to be guilty, unless she could prove she was innocent. The trial should have gone smoothly for the English.

But Joan had the help of her voices and the inspiration of clever Saint Catherine. From the very beginning, her words startled the learned men. "Consider well what you are about," she warned Cauchon, "for in truth I am sent from God and you are putting yourself in great peril."

There was little light and no escape in the castle tower where Joan was held at Rouen.

On February 21, 1430, Joan's guard, Jean Massieu, led her from her cell, across the courtyard, and up into the royal chapel for her first hearing. She begged to be allowed to stop in a side chapel along the way to take communion, or simply to pray. Massieu could not allow that, but he did pause and allow her to pray a moment in the side chapel's doorway. He managed to stop with her outside that

Inquisitions

Starting in 1184, the Catholic Church established a series of organizations known as inquisitions, dedicated to trying and punishing heretics. The inquisitions were extremely unfair, often using torture to extract confessions and giving the accused little chance to defend themselves. The most notorious was the Spanish Inquisition, founded in 1478. (The word *inquistion* can also refer to an individual trial.)

The Gospels are the first four books of the New Testament. This German edition is a rare work of art.

door every day of her three-month trial.

Once Joan was in the main chapel, d'Estivet asked her to swear on the Gospels that she would truthfully answer all his questions. Every morning, she refused, saying that there were things her voices had told her never to say. She told her judges they could cut off her head before she would reveal what God had said to her. Sometimes she would say that she needed a week to discuss with the saints whether she could answer.

In response to questions about her faith, Joan said her mother had taught her all she knew about religion. Cauchon quickly asked her to recite the Lord's Prayer, one of the most well-known prayers in Christianity. He figured that an illiterate country girl would get confused as she prayed aloud, especially standing among all these priests, with half a dozen scribes taking notes. Everybody knew that witches could not say the Lords Prayer. Joan turned the question around to her own advantage. "I will not," she said, "unless you hear me in

> ### GRACE
> For Christians, grace is a state in which one's sins have been forgiven by God.

confession." They both knew that a priest could not divulge what he heard in confession—and he couldn't refuse a request for confession either. Cauchon changed the subject.

"Are you in God's grace?" she was asked one day. It was another trick question. If she said yes, she would be claiming that her sins had been forgiven. This was a judgment that only God could make. If she said no, she would be admitting to sin.

"If I am not, may God put me there," she answered. "If I am, may God keep me there. I would be the most miserable person in the world if I knew I were not in God's grace."

Joan's bravery and sharp tongue pleased the crowds who squeezed into the chapel. Admiring stories of her wit spread fast. Bishop Cauchon had to stop that. He moved the trial into a small room and banned all onlookers. The scribes still took notes, so we know today what was said.

Though she is bound in chains and surrounded by enemies, Joan looks very dignified in this 1819 painting of her prison cell.

Exhausted by endless questioning, Joan begged the well-spoken Saint Catherine for help keeping her wits under the pressure.

Over and over, Joan was asked about her clothing. The voices told her to wear it, she insisted. It was to guard her virginity. And in prison, she needed that protection more than ever.

Many questions focused on the Fairy Tree in her village and the ancient springtime rites she had performed there. Though it was simply child's play, the men made it seem like a form of devil worship.

The inquisitors tried to trap her by asking about her visions. The church held that saints were not physical beings, though Joan had said "I saw them with my own eyes as I now see you." They asked if the saints had hair and Joan replied, "It is good to know they did." Did they smell nice? Did she kiss or embrace them? To each of these questions, Joan answered yes. It gave the inquisitors another juicy angle to follow. What part of them did you embrace?

Joan answered that she embraced them at their knees or feet, as one does with a superior. The judges wanted more. They asked if the bodies felt solid and warm. Joan said, "I could not embrace them without feeling or touching them." Looking for more, they asked if the archangel Michael had hair. "Why should it be cut off?" Joan answered. Another priest asked if Michael appeared to be naked. Her answer made many laugh. "Do you think God could not afford to clothe him?"

But the trial was deadly serious. To get Joan to stop answering playfully, her judges took her down to a torture room. Surrounded by whips, racks, and other cruel devices designed to pull and tear bodies apart, Joan was reminded that other methods could be used to get answers from people. Then she was led back to her cell to think about it.

Day after day, the questioning went on. Joan was exhausted, just as the English hoped. She got confused in her answers. Sometimes she said things she didn't mean to. The clerics made a distinction between the church on earth and the church in heaven.

Prisoners in a torture chamber like this would often say anything, true or not, to get the pain to stop.

In this illuminated manuscript, the Bishop Cauchon is pictured questioning Joan of Arc, all within an oversized letter A.

When Joan was questioned on this subject, she got herself in trouble. She insisted that she listened only to God and Jesus and the saints; the church in heaven. But all the men around her represented the church on earth. They wanted everyone to submit to them. Most importantly, they wanted Joan to submit, and she wouldn't.

Finally, Cauchon listed 70 charges that had a chance of being proven. They were read to Joan and narrowed down to 12 or so. Joan was taken out to a cemetery near the castle where two wooden platforms had been raised. On one stood a tall stake surrounded by firewood. "Do you repent?" the judges demanded. "Will you give up men's clothes? Do you promise to give up fighting? Will you submit to the church on earth? Or do you want to burn to death—now?"

Joan gazed at the stake. She shuddered, and mumbled her agreement. Then her judges presented her with a list of charges that she could not read. Rather than signing her name, she drew a cross in a circle. Many think she was purposefully using her old code, signaling that she meant the

REPENT

To repent is to feel sorry for offending God by sinning, and to vow to sin no more.

opposite of what was written on the paper.

Cauchon triumphantly read her sentence: life in prison. Joan quickly asked to be taken out of the hands of the English and put into a church prison. Instead, she was given a dress to wear and taken right back to the cell where she'd lived for five months. Sometime in the next few days, her clothes were stolen while she slept. She was left with nothing but men's clothes. Her choice was to wander past the bored, lusty guards in nothing but a thin cotton slip, or put on some clothes for protection. Eventually, she dressed as a boy again.

She was arrested immediately. The church allows a heretic to repent. Joan had repented and saved herself. Now she had relapsed, choosing her old evil ways over the church's righteous path.

Joan was horrified to be sent back to the same cell and the same untrustworthy guards after she'd signed her confession.

Every artist shows Joan's death differently. Here she is shown in a red dress, like those worn by medieval brides.

Later, Bishop Cauchon met his colleague, the Earl of Warwick, in a courtyard of the castle. "Be of good cheer," said the bishop. "It is done."

Only three of the twenty churchmen agreed that Joan should be killed immediately as a relapsed heretic. The rest felt she should have another chance or have the charges explained better in case she hadn't understood. The only judges with the power to sentence were Cauchon and le Maître. They decided to burn Joan the next morning.

At dawn on May 30, two doctors went to Joan's cell to tell her. For the first time, Joan fell to pieces. She sobbed and wailed. "I would rather be beheaded seven times than burned!" she cried. Surprisingly, she was allowed to take communion at last.

"Bishop, I die through you," she said when Cauchon appeared in her cell. The sound of an excited crowd floated through the castle.

Joan, weeping, dressed in a long black shift. A pointed cap with the words "Heretic, relapsed, apostate, idolater" written on it was perched on her shaved head. As the executioner's cart carried her to the old market, she glanced at the stake. A large sign above it read: "Joan the Maid, liar, pernicious, seducer of the people, diviner, superstitious, blasphemer of God, presumptuous, misbelieving in the faith of Jesus Christ, idolater, cruel, dissolute invoker of devils, apostate, schismatic and heretic."

She could not read the insults. She could barely listen to the sermon preached at her. Joan fell on her knees, loudly praying for forgiveness as she forgave all who condemned her. She asked that they pray for her, too. Then she asked for a cross. An English bystander made her a cross of sticks. She kissed it and pressed it to her chest.

A churchman ran for a cross she could watch as the fire was lit. "Jesus!" she called out. "Jesus!" When her cries stopped, the fire was raked aside so the crowd could see by her naked, charred body that she had not escaped death. Then the fire was relit and oil was added to burn away any souvenirs that people might take home and keep as relics of the saintly Maid of Orléans.

Sometimes executioners stabbed prisoners to spare them the pain of fire. Joan had only prayer to protect her.

14

Justice at Last

Joan was gone. All across France, people grieved. The English had tried their best to discredit the Maid, but the French had rallied under her banner. They had felt the sweet taste of patriotism. She had given them a king and the idea of a strong, noble France.

Throughout the country, stories and legends about Joan continued to multiply. A pure white dove had miraculously flown from the fire as her soul left her body. She had commanded the weather itself. Her touch had healed a dead child. Her heart had survived the fire untouched.

In England, the stories were different. The playwright William

Years after Joan's death, Charles VII visited Rouen. This may have encouraged him to reopen her trial.

Shakespeare called her a "foul fiend." Joan was the topic of horror stories and nasty jokes. Bishop Cauchon was hailed as a hero.

Any letter from Charles VII was sealed with wax. This royal stamp was pressed into the wax while it was still hot.

Battles between the French and English were still being fought, but the tide had turned. The Duke of Bedford tried to have the nine-year-old Henry VI crowned at Reims. But Bedford didn't honor ancient French traditions so the French didn't accept Henry. They had a king. More than that, they had a country. Charles VII reigned for almost forty years, and slowly did much to restore peace and justice to France.

Even French clerics began to show independence. They stopped sending as much money to the pope. Instead they put it toward healing their wounded communities and rebuilding chapels and cathedrals all over the country.

Bedford died and the citizens of Paris gladly handed their city over to the true French king. French forces fought as Joan had taught them, fearlessly and decisively. Village by village, they took back their country.

In 1453, twenty-two years after Joan's death, the English were forced out of France forever.

When Rouen fell, King Charles had taken possession of one of the records of Joan's trial. He and his counselors read it carefully. Everyone knew Joan was the force behind his

The king got to study this transcript of Joan's trial. Today, it is in the hands of a museum, along with four others.

coronation. Her conviction as a heretic was an enormous blot on his reputation.

With his support, a new investigation began under Inquisitor Jean Bréhal and another churchman, Guillaume d'Estouteville, to clear Joan's name.

The king couldn't undo Joan's conviction by himself. Her crime had been tried in church courts. Churchmen would have to admit that they'd acted in bad faith when they'd found her guilty. Luckily for Charles, the old pope had died. The new pope, Nicholas V, wanted good relations with this new, independent France. He didn't want to lose all control over the French church. He needed Charles's support, so he agreed to a rehabilitation trial for Joan.

Both the pope and Charles granted amnesty to

Bloodletting

The practice of bloodletting, or releasing blood from patients, has a long history in medicine. Doctors in Ancient Greece believed that the balance of fluids in a human body affected its health. Too much of any one fluid, including blood, caused disease. Doctors used knives or leeches to drain off extra blood, in an attempt to cure sick patients. The practice finally fell out of favor in the 19th century.

all who testified. That way, witnesses were free to say things against church or state authorities without fear of punishment.

Inquisitor Bréhal began preliminary interviews. Cauchon had died in the course of a bloodletting. The body of d'Estevet, Joan's prosecutor, had been found drowned in an open sewer. But the remaining churchmen from Joan's trial in Rouen agreed that it had been political, designed to discredit Charles as having been crowned by a sorceress.

Joan's mother was 82, yet she limped into the cathedral of Notre Dame in Paris to assure Bréhal that her daughter "went frequently to church . . . and gave herself to fasting and to prayer with great devotion and fervor."

The inquisitions were known more for condemning people than clearing their names. Here, a Grand Inquisitor meets with the pope.

Nullification

Once a judge has pronounced a guilty verdict in a court, it is law. Only a second trial, which re-examines the evidence and the procedures of the first, can alter this decision. If the judge in this second trial decides a mistake was made, he can reverse (or nullify) the first verdict. Although the details of the procedure vary from country to country, this basic legal principle is as true in our day as it was in Joan's.

Over a year or two, Inquisitor Bréhal compiled a list of 27 issues to examine. It included the hatred the Englishmen had expressed for Joan and all the ways they had bent court rules. Joan's treatment in jail made the list. So did her loyalty to the church. Joan's claims of divine voices and her attitude towards authority needed re-examination, too.

In Rome, Bréhal presented his list to yet another new pope. Calixtus III approved, and appointed three commissioners to act in his name at a formal trial of nullification. Now the inquisitor began calling witnesses from all over France. Each of them would be asked what they knew about the truth of those 27 statements. Then a new verdict would be issued.

One hundred and fifteen witnesses testified. In Domrémy, Joan's childhood friends Hauviette, Mengette, and Michael Lebuin shared their memories. They were all in their midforties now, as Joan would have been if she'd survived. "From my youth," Hauviette said, "I knew Joan the Maid, who was born at Domrémy of Jacques d'Ark and Isabellette, spouses, honest farmers and true Catholics of good reputation." The churchwarden, Joan's godparents, a next door neighbor—all swore to her piety throughout childhood.

Bréhal traced Joan's life, taking testimony from the kind people who had sheltered her, the soldiers she had commanded, the courtiers she had befriended, and still others from castles and courts, abbeys and armories. In the end, all the evidence suggested that Joan had given truthful testimony. Though the reality of her voices could not be proven, everything she said about them was consistent throughout her short life. And many people who had testified against her admitted that they had lied.

On July 7, 1456, an announcement was made in Rouen proclaiming that the first trial had been flawed. Joan was not guilty. A copy of the transcript was publicly shredded. Ceremonies followed. A solemn service was held in Rouen's Old Marketplace, where Joan had burned to death 25 years earlier. Across France, people wept for their little Maid. She had been killed only for political gain. Many now saw her as a martyr.

With Joan's record cleared, French people could once again rally around her piety and love for France.

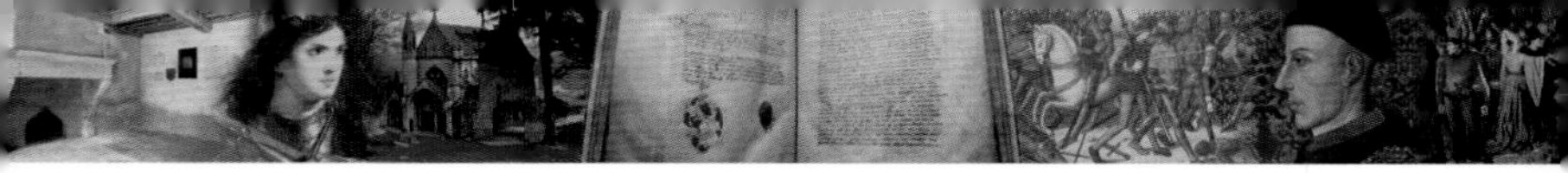

15

Joan Today

The world's fascination with Joan of Arc never died out. For hundreds of years, books, paintings, tapestries, and statues of the Maid of Orléans celebrated her faith and courage. Joan was revered, especially in France. Orléans held festivals and celebrations in her honor, almost as if she were a saint.

Joan appears here on a Catholic devotional card. The halo represents her status as a saint.

In 1869, the Bishop of Orléans wrote to the pope to nominate Joan for sainthood. The process of being officially recognized as a saint by the Catholic Church is a long and formal one. Once Joan passed years of investigations, proving that she had lived an outstandingly holy life, the church began to focus on her special qualifications for sainthood. The church sees it as a sign of saintliness if a person displayed heroic virtue. The performance of a miracle is another such sign. If one of these can be proven beyond a shadow of a doubt, the candidate can be beatified, earning the title Blessed. Joan was a virtuous hero to thousands of French people. The Maid of Orléans became Blessed Joan of Arc under Pope Pius X in 1909.

Years of further research had to be conducted before she could be officially canonized as a saint or "Friend of God." On May 16, 1920,

Although he declared Joan the soldier to be a saint, Benedict XV took a strongly antiwar stance during World War I.

Blessed Joan became Saint Joan of Arc in a formal ceremony under Pope Benedict XV. French people celebrated in the streets. Masses were said in churches around the world. The Maid had been dead for 490 years, but a new chapter of her life in the church was just beginning.

The church assigns every saint a feast day. It is a time to focus on how the saint lived his or her faith on earth. The feast of Saint Joan of Arc is celebrated every year on May 30, the day she died. Her symbol is the sword. Even if one is not a Catholic, or a believer in sainthood, Joan can be an excellent role model—a courageous young woman, an effective military leader, and a powerful self-advocate.

The Maid of Orléans is the patron saint of soldiers, many of whom wear her medal to help them remember

Parades in medieval costume are only part of the annual Joan of Arc celebrations in Orléans.

how valiantly she fought while still keeping her faith. Today, a Catholic soldier might ask for Joan's help before going into battle, hoping for a little of her courage. Because she kept her dignity while imprisoned, she is the patron saint of prisoners as well. She might have lost her fight for freedom, but in the eyes of believers, she triumphed in the end.

The country of France also claims Joan of Arc as a patron saint. Even nonreligious citizens see her as a patriotic hero. The French government declared May 8 to be a national holiday dedicated to her memory. French churches and neighborhoods still celebrate that day with special foods and greetings. It helps the people remember the history of their beloved nation, along with its religious roots.

In 1874, long before Joan was canonized, a magnificent statue of her was erected in Paris. It shows Joan in battle, riding her horse, banner raised high as she leads her countrymen in a charge.

PATRON SAINT

A patron saint is a saint with a special connection to a place or group of people.

In 1958, the people of France gave a copy of the statue to the city of New Orleans, Louisiana,

in thanks for America's help in World War II. Twenty-seven years later, the statue was given a gleaming coat of gold. At the base, it reads: "JOAN OF ARC / MAID OF ORLEANS."

The inspiration that powered that slender teenage girl more than 500 years ago still moves us today. After Hurricane Katrina devastated New Orleans in 2005, people asked "Is Joan still standing?" "Did anything happen to the statue?" "Was 'Joanie on the Pony' swept away?"

The next day, the local newspaper printed photographs of the golden statue on the front page for all to see. Joan of Arc still rode tall, strong, and proud. The citizens of New Orleans found her image deeply reassuring. She seemed to be rallying the whole city to fight its way back from its misfortune. The photographer was right when he called The Maid of Orléans a "beacon of hope."

Impervious even to hurricanes, the Maid of Orléans still rides tall in New Orleans, Louisiana.

Events in the Life of Joan of Arc

Spring 1428
Joan's parents arrange a marriage. Joan refuses, vowing never to wed.

February 1429
At Vaucouleurs, Baudricourt gives Joan horses and soldiers.

May 8, 1429
The English surrender Orléans to Joan and the French forces.

1412 or 1413
Joan of Arc is born in the farming village of Domrémy, France.

March 6, 1429
Joan identifies the dauphin at Chinon and gains his trust.

June 8, 1429
Joan embarks on her Loire campaign to clear the path to Reims.

1424
Joan hears voices. They tell her to crown the dauphin king of France.

April 29, 1429
Joan arrives at English-held Orléans. Battle begins five days later.

April 1429
Joan gets her banner and armor and joins the armies at Blois.

May 1428
Robert de Baudricourt refuses to help Joan meet the dauphin.

June 18, 1429
Joan's armies crush a huge English/ Burgundian force at the Battle of Patay.

June 25, 1429
Joan meets the dauphin at Gien and convinces him to march to Reims.

May 24, 1431
Threatened with death, Joan signs a confession, but returns to prison.

May 28, 1431
Caught wearing men's clothes again, Joan is declared a relapsed heretic.

May 30, 1431
Joan is burned at the stake in the Old Marketplace at Rouen.

July 17, 1429
Charles VII is crowned at Reims cathedral with Joan by his side.

July 7, 1456
A new trial declares Joan innocent.

May 23, 1430
Burgundians capture Joan outside the gate at Compiègne.

January 9, 1431
Joan's trial begins, run by pro-English clerics who are paid by England.

November 1430
Burgundians turn Joan over to the English for ransom.

May 16, 1920
Joan is canonized by Pope Benedict XV, becoming Saint Joan of Arc.

Bibliography

Brooks, Polly Schoyer. *Beyond the Myth: The Story of Joan of Arc*. New York: J.P. Lippincott, 1990.

Hobbins, Daniel. *The Trial of Joan of Arc*. Trans. Daniel Hobbins. Cambridge, MA: Harvard University Press, 2005.

Nash-Marshall, Siobhan. *Joan of Arc: A Spiritual Biography*. New York: The Crossroad Publishing Company, 1999.

Pernoud, Regine and Marie Veronique Clin. *Joan of Arc: Her Story*. Trans. Jeremy duQuesnay Adams. New York: St. Martin's Press, 1998.

Sackville-West, Vita. *Saint Joan of Arc*. New York: Grove Press, 1936.

Works Cited

p.8 "Jesus!" *Beyond the Myth: The Story of Joan of Arc*, page 148

p.9 "We are all ruined . . ." *Beyond the Myth: The Story of Joan of Arc*, page 116

p.14 "received the sacrament . . ." *Joan of Arc: Her Story*, page 156

p.24 "Joan caught up with me and . . ." *Joan of Arc: Her Story*, page 161

p.25 "Often when we were playing . . ." *Joan of Arc: Her Story*, page 163

p.29 "Once she told me . . ." *Joan of Arc: Her Story*, page 163

p.37 "He shall have no help . . ." *Beyond the Myth: The Story of Joan of Arc*, page 33

p.39 "God give you life, gentle king . . ." *Joan of Arc: Her Story*, page 22

p.40 "I often saw her . . ." *Joan of Arc: Her Story*, page 25

p.42 "the city of Orléans . . ." *Joan of Arc: Her Story*, page 29

p.45 "It would be rusted . . ." *Joan of Arc: Her Story*, page 37

p.49 "King of England . . ." *Joan of Arc: Her Story*, page 33

p.51 "Are you the one . . ." *Joan of Arc: Her Story*, page 40

p.58 "Fight for France!" *Beyond the Myth: The Story of Joan of Arc*, page 65

p.60 "Whether you wish it or not . . ." *Joan of Arc: Her Story*, page 45

p.70 "bowed as deeply as she . . ." *Joan of Arc: Her Story*, page 53

p.71 "Do not hold a council . . ." *Joan of Arc: Her Story*, page 57

p.71 "Lady, have no fear . . ." *Saint Joan of Arc*, page 130

p.73 "Are you afraid, gentle duke?" *Joan of Arc: Her Story*, page 59

p.73 "Up, up, my friends!" *Joan of Arc: Her Story*, page 60

For Further Study

For many helpful links to Joan of Arc documents and information, visit the Web site of the Saint Joan of Arc Center: http://www.stjoan-center.com/

The Joan of Arc Archive contains an amazing wealth of Joan information, including a full-length online biography, as well as book and movie reviews: http://archive.joan-of-arc.org/

In Rouen, France, a museum stands near where Joan was burned at the stake. Visit them online at: http://perso.orange.fr/musee.jeannedarc/indexanglais.htm

The gold-plated statue "The Maid of Orleans" stands proudly at the corner of St. Philip and Decatur in the French Quarter of New Orleans, Louisiana. It is an exact copy of the 1880 Emmanuel Frémiet statue located in Paris.

To explore life in the Middle Ages, spend some time at Minnesota State University's interactive online museum: http://www.mnsu.edu/emuseum/history/middleages/

Index

Acknowledgments

The author wishes to thank Laura Ann Coyle, PhD, founder of Curator-at-Large, and curator of the national touring exhibit Joan of Arc: Medieval Maiden to Modern Saint for vetting this text. Profound thanks as well to John Searcy, superb DK editor.

Picture Credits

About the Author

Kathleen Kudlinski is the author of more than 30 children's books, including a biography of Rachel Carson, a historical novel about the San Francisco Earthquake, and *Boy, Were We Wrong About Dinosaurs!*, a science picture book. She lives in Guilford, Connecticut, and Springfield, Vermont, with her husband, Hank.

Other DK Biographies you'll enjoy:

Charles Darwin
David C. King
ISBN 978-0-7566-2554-2 paperback
ISBN 978-0-7566-2555-9 hardcover

Princess Diana
Joanne Mattern
ISBN 978-0-7566-1614-4 paperback
ISBN 978-0-7566-1613-7 hardcover

Amelia Earhart
Tanya Lee Stone
ISBN 978-0-7566-2552-8 paperback
ISBN 978-0-7566-2553-5 hardcover

Albert Einstein
Frieda Wishinsky
ISBN 978-0-7566-1247-4 paperback
ISBN 978-0-7566-1248-1 hardcover

Benjamin Franklin
Stephen Krensky
ISBN 978-0-7566-3528-2 paperback
ISBN 978-0-7566-3529-9 hardcover

Gandhi
Amy Pastan
ISBN 978-0-7566-2111-7 paperback
ISBN 978-0-7566-2112-4 hardcover

Harry Houdini
Vicki Cobb
ISBN 978-0-7566-1245-0 paperback
ISBN 978-0-7566-1246-7 hardcover

Helen Keller
Leslie Garrett
ISBN 978-0-7566-0339-7 paperback
ISBN 978-0-7566-0488-2 hardcover

John F. Kennedy
Howard S. Kaplan
ISBN 978-0-7566-0340-3 paperback
ISBN 978-0-7566-0489-9 hardcover

Martin Luther King, Jr.
Amy Pastan
ISBN 978-0-7566-0342-7 paperback
ISBN 978-0-7566-0491-2 hardcover

Abraham Lincoln
Tanya Lee Stone
ISBN 978-0-7566-0834-7 paperback
ISBN 978-0-7566-0833-0 hardcover

Nelson Mandela
Lenny Hort & Laaren Brown
ISBN 978-0-7566-2109-4 paperback
ISBN 978-0-7566-2110-0 hardcover

Annie Oakley
Chuck Wills
ISBN 978-0-7566-2997-7 paperback
ISBN 978-0-7566-2986-1 hardcover

Pelé
Jim Buckley
ISBN 978-0-7566-2987-8 paperback
ISBN 978-0-7566-2996-0 hardcover

Eleanor Roosevelt
Kem Knapp Sawyer
ISBN 978-0-7566-1496-6 paperback
ISBN 978-0-7566-1495-9 hardcover

George Washington
Lenny Hort
ISBN 978-0-7566-0835-4 paperback
ISBN 978-0-7566-0832-3 hardcover

Look what the critics are saying about DK Biography!

"...highly readable, worthwhile overviews for young people..." —*Booklist*

"This new series from the inimitable DK Publishing brings together the usual brilliant photography with a historian's approach to biography subjects." —*Ingram Library Services*